THE
POWER
of
FAITH

DEREK PRINCE

THE
POWER
of
FAITH

ENTERING INTO THE FULLNESS OF GOD'S POSSIBILITIES

WHITAKER
HOUSE

THE POWER OF FAITH:
Entering into the Fullness of God's Possibilities
Revised and Expanded Edition (formerly titled *Faith to Live By*)

Derek Prince Ministries
P. O. Box 19501
Charlotte, North Carolina 28219-9501
www.derekprince.org
https://www.facebook.com/dpmlegacy/

ISBN: 978-1-64123-022-3 • Ebook ISBN: 978-1-64123-027-8
Printed in the United States of America
© 1977, 2018 by Derek Prince Ministries—International

Whitaker House • 1030 Hunt Valley Circle • New Kensington, PA 15068
www.whitakerhouse.com

The Library of Congress has cataloged the first trade paperback edition as follows:
Prince, Derek.
Faith to live by / by Derek Prince.
p.   cm.
ISBN 0-88368-519-1 (trade paper)
1. Faith.   I. Title.
BV4637.P75   1997
234'.23—dc21   97-46142

3 4 5 6 7 8 9 10 11 12 **LLJ** 26 25 24 23 22 21 20 19 18

CONTENTS

FAITH IS THE CHANNEL THAT
MAKES GOD'S POSSIBILITIES
AVAILABLE TO US.

1

FAITH VERSUS SIGHT

Faith! Who can fully measure or express the potential represented by that short, simple word? Perhaps the clearest way to bring faith's potential into focus is to examine two statements made by Jesus:

> *With God all things are possible.* (Matthew 19:26)

> *All things are possible to him who believes.* (Mark 9:23)

In each of these statements, we find the words *"all things are possible."* In the first passage, these words are applied to God; in the second, they are applied to the one who believes. We can easily accept that all things are possible with God. Can we equally accept that all things are possible to the one who believes? This is what Jesus is saying to us.

What does this mean in practical terms? It means that, through faith, the things that are possible to God are made equally possible to the one who believes. Faith is the channel that makes God's possibilities available to us. Is it any wonder that the Bible, from beginning to end, consistently emphasizes the unique and supreme importance of faith?

FAITH IS THE UNDERLYING
REALITY OF THINGS HOPED FOR.

PROBLEMS OF TRANSLATION

Before we go any further with our study, I need to clear up a linguistic misunderstanding that often causes difficulties in comprehending faith. In English, we have two different word forms for faith: a noun, *faith*, and a verb, *believe*. The connection between these two words is not always obvious. As a result, preachers sometimes try to make a distinction between "believing" and "having faith." However, there is no basis for this distinction in the original Greek of the New Testament.

In Greek, the basic word for faith is *pistis*, and the word for believe is *pisteuo*. We see that the verb is formed directly from the noun. The stem of each word is made up of the same four letters—*pist*. As far as the Bible is concerned, believing is exercising faith. Conversely, exercising faith is believing.

When we look at the words that express the opposite of faith, we again find a difference between English and Greek. In English, the opposite of faith is unbelief. We have no such word as "unfaith." But, in Greek, there is a direct connection between faith and its opposite. Faith is *pistis*; unbelief is *apistia*. (In Greek, the negative prefix *a* corresponds to the English prefix *un*.) The same four-letter stem, *pist*, occurs in both Greek words: faith, *pistis*, and unbelief, *apistia*.

Also connected with this four-letter stem *pist*, we have the adjective *pistos*, which means faithful, believing. From this, the negative prefix *a* gives us the opposite adjective, *apistos*, which means unfaithful, unbelieving.

For the sake of clarity, we will set these five words side by side in two parallel columns:

	Greek	English
Noun:	*pistis*	faith
Noun:	*apistia*	unbelief
Adjective:	*pistos*	faithful, believing
Adjective:	*apistos*	unfaithful, unbelieving
Verb:	*pisteuo*	believe

FAITH CONNECTS US TO TWO
ETERNAL, INVISIBLE REALITIES:
GOD AND HIS WORD.

We see that all five Greek words are visibly linked by the stem *pist* that is part of each of them. Altogether, these five words occur almost six hundred times in the original text of the New Testament. On this basis alone, it is clear that these words represent a theme that is central to the Bible's total revelation.

FAITH DEFINED

The eleventh chapter of Hebrews deals exclusively with the theme of faith. Its opening verse provides us with a definition of faith as the term is used in the Bible: *"Now faith is the substance of things hoped for, the evidence of things not seen"* (Hebrews 11:1 KJV).

This verse tells us two main truths about faith. First, *"faith is the substance of things hoped for."* Faith is so real that it is actually called a substance. The Greek word translated *"substance"* is *hupostasis*. It literally means "that which stands under or provides the basis for."

The same word occurs in Hebrews 1:3, where we are told that Jesus is *"the exact representation of His* [the Father's] *nature."* The word here translated *"nature"* is *hupostasis*. The meaning is that God the Father is the eternal, invisible, underlying reality of which Jesus Christ the Son is the visible expression. Applying this meaning to Hebrews 11:1, we may say that faith is the underlying reality of things hoped for. Faith is real; faith is a substance.

Second, faith is *"the evidence of things not seen"* (Hebrews 11:1 KJV). The *New American Standard Bible* says *"the conviction of things not seen."* Regardless of which translation we prefer, the vital point is that faith deals with things we cannot see. Faith relates to the invisible.

Two verses later, the writer again stressed faith's relationship to the invisible:

> By faith we understand that the worlds were prepared by the word of God, so that what is seen was not made out of things which are visible.   (Hebrews 11:3)

FIRST WE MUST BELIEVE;
THEN WE WILL SEE.

The writer pointed out that there is a contrast between the things that are seen and the things that are not seen, between the visible and the invisible. Our senses connect us to the visible world, to *"what is seen."* But faith takes us behind the visible to the invisible—to the underlying reality by which the whole universe was formed: the reality of the Word of God.

Thus, faith relates to two eternal, invisible realities: to God Himself and to His Word. Biblical faith has only these two objects. In secular speech, of course, we speak of faith in many other contexts. We can talk about having faith in the economy, in a medicine, or in a political leader. But faith is not used that way in the Bible. In Scripture, faith is related solely and exclusively to these two realities we cannot see with the natural eye: to God and to God's Word.

BY FAITH, NOT BY SIGHT

Paul brought out the opposition between faith and sight in 2 Corinthians 5:7: *"For we walk by faith, not by sight."* If we walk by sight, we do not need faith. If we walk by faith, we do not need sight. Each excludes the other.

This is contrary to our natural way of thinking. The world says, "Seeing is believing." But the Bible reverses the order: first we must believe, then we will see. Because this principle is so important for us to grasp, we will look at several passages of Scripture that illustrate it. In Psalm 27:13, David said, *"I would have despaired unless I had believed that I would see the goodness of the LORD in the land of the living."* Which came first, believing or seeing? Believing. What was true for David is true for all of us. If we cannot believe that we will see the goodness of the Lord, we will despair. What keeps us from despairing is not what we see, but what we believe.

This corresponds with the statement made about Moses in Hebrews 11:27: *"By faith he left Egypt, not fearing the wrath of the king; for he endured, as seeing Him who is unseen."* Nothing about

Moses's visible circumstances at that time could have given him any hope or encouragement. But in spite of all that was against him, he endured because he was able to see the unseen. How did he do this? By faith. Faith enables us to see the unseen and thus enables us to endure when the visible world offers us no hope or encouragement.

Another example of walking by faith rather than by sight is found in John chapter 11, which is the record of Jesus raising Lazarus from the dead:

> *Jesus said, "Remove the stone." Martha, the sister of the deceased, said to Him, "Lord, by this time there will be a stench, for he has been dead four days." Jesus said to her, "Did I not say to you, if you believe, you will see the glory of God?"*
> (John 11:39–40)

What Jesus asked of Martha, He asks of all who desire to see the glory of God. We must believe that we will see. We do not see first, then believe. We believe first; then, as a result of believing, we see. Faith comes before sight.

Here, then, is the basic conflict between the old nature and the new nature. The old nature demands to *see*, since the old nature lives by the senses. God has to deliver us from that old nature and that old way of life and bring us to a new nature and a new way of life. Then we can say, "I am content *not* to see. I do not walk by sight, but by faith."

In the book of 2 Corinthians, we are challenged once more by the contrast between the visible and the invisible:

> *For momentary, light affliction is producing for us an eternal weight of glory far beyond all comparison, while we look not at the things which are seen, but at the things which are not seen; for the things which are seen are temporal, but the things which are not seen are eternal.* (2 Corinthians 4:17–18)

Paul's language in these verses contains a deliberate paradox. He spoke about looking at things that are not seen. How can we do this? There is only one way—by faith!

There is great significance in the word *"while"*: *"while we look not at the things which are seen."* It stresses the same lesson Moses learned in his test of endurance. He learned that, in the providence of God, affliction serves a useful purpose for believers. It forms and strengthens our character and prepares us for the eternal glory that lies ahead. But the lesson that the word *"while"* teaches us is this: Affliction serves us only while we keep our eyes on the invisible realm. If we lose sight of it by becoming preoccupied with the world of time and of the senses, we are no longer able to receive the benefits that affliction is intended to provide for us.

So we are caught between two worlds: the temporal and the eternal. The temporal is what we can see; we contact it with our senses. But the eternal is the world God wants us to be at home in. And we can be at home in that world by only one means: faith. Faith is the one thing that connects us to the unseen realities of God and His Word.

SUMMARY

Faith lifts us above the realm of our own abilities and makes God's possibilities available to us. Faith connects us to two unseen realities: God and His Word. As we maintain a relationship with God through faith, we are enabled to endure and to overcome the tests and the hardships that confront us in our daily lives. In turn, these trials become opportunities for God to reveal to us (and others) His goodness and His glory.

There is an ongoing tension between faith and sight. Our old nature is at home in the world of the senses, and it demands to see. As Christians, we need to cultivate the new nature, which trusts God and His Word without demanding other evidence.

A PERSON WHO
TRULY BELIEVES WILL BE
CHANGED BY WHAT HE BELIEVES.

2

FAITH VERSUS HOPE

In chapter one, we examined the difference between faith and sight—between believing and seeing. In this chapter, we will examine the difference between faith and hope. Herein lies one of the greatest sources of misunderstanding among Christians today. Many Christians are disappointed and frustrated with prayer because they do not receive what they think they should. Often it is because they are praying in hope, but not in faith. The results promised by God to faith are not promised to hope.

What is the difference between faith and hope? How can we tell them apart?

FAITH IS IN THE HEART

The first essential difference is that faith is in the heart, while hope is in the mind. In Romans 10:10, Paul said, *"For with the heart man believeth unto righteousness"* (KJV). True biblical faith originates in the heart. In this verse, it is expressed by the verb *believe*, and it is followed by the preposition *"unto,"* indicating the result that it produces: *"righteousness."* The word *unto* implies motion or transition of some kind. Faith is never static. It always expresses itself in motion, change, and activity. A person who truly believes will be changed by what he believes.

FAITH IS THE ONLY
SOLID BASIS FOR HOPE.

On the other hand, a person who merely accepts truth with his intellect can remain unchanged by it. Mental acceptance of truth is not faith. To produce faith, truth must penetrate beyond the conscious mind into the inner center and source of life, which is called the heart. Truth received intellectually by the mind may be sterile and ineffective, but truth received by faith into the heart is always dynamic and life-changing.

In Proverbs 4:23, Solomon warned us, *"Watch over your heart with all diligence, for from it flow the springs of life."* Everything that finally decides the course of our lives proceeds from our hearts. True biblical faith proceeds from the heart and determines the way we live. It is not a mere intellectual concept, entertained by the mind; it is a real, active force at work in the heart.

However, God does not leave the mind without its proper provision. Faith at work in the heart produces hope in the mind. We see this in the definition of faith we have already examined in Hebrews 11:1: *"Faith is the substance of things hoped for"* (kjv). Faith in the heart is the substance, the underlying reality. This provides a valid, scriptural basis for the hope that we entertain in our minds.

In 1 Thessalonians 5:8, Paul mentioned the different areas of our personalities that are affected by faith and those that are affected by hope: *"But since we are of the day, let us be sober, having put on the breastplate of faith and love, and as a helmet, the hope of salvation."* Faith and love are the breastplate, and the breastplate protects the heart. Hope is the helmet, and it protects the head, or the mind.

In distinguishing faith from hope, I do not mean to belittle hope. Hope, in the biblical sense, is a confident expectation of good—a steady, persistent optimism. Hope protects our minds. Every Christian should wear this helmet of hope twenty-four hours a day. If we lay aside the helmet and begin to dwell on negative thoughts and gloomy forebodings, our minds are vulnerable to Satan's subtle attacks.

FAITH IS IN THE PRESENT,
WHILE HOPE IS IN THE FUTURE.

True Christian optimism is not fanciful or unrealistic. It is not mere wishful thinking. Optimism must be based firmly and exclusively on the statements and promises of Scripture. For example, in Romans 8:28, we are told, *"And we know that God causes all things to work together for good to those who love God, to those who are called according to His purpose."* If God is working all things together for our good, what room is left for anything but optimism?

However, in applying this verse to our lives, we first need to make sure that we are meeting its conditions. Do we truly love God? Are we seeking to fulfill His purpose for our lives? If so, then God is working all things—every event, every situation—together for our good. This leaves only one attitude of mind that we can logically adopt: optimism. In light of this, for a Christian to be a pessimist is, in fact, a denial of his faith.

This example confirms what has already been said: Faith is the only solid basis for hope. We must first truly believe what Romans 8:28 tells us—that all things are working together for our good. If we believe this, we have no alternative but to hope. But if we do not believe this, then our hope has no solid basis.

So we see there are two forms of hope. Outwardly, they are similar, but they are different in one vital respect: one is based on faith, and one is not. One form of hope is based on genuine faith within the heart, and it is therefore valid. Its expectation will, at the right time, be fulfilled. The other form of hope is within the mind alone, lacking any basis of genuine faith within the heart, and therefore has no scriptural validity. More likely than not, it is doomed to disappointment. Until we have learned to distinguish between these two forms of hope, we will always be in danger of entertaining hopes that will never be fulfilled.

FAITH IS IN THE PRESENT

Therefore, the first essential difference between faith and hope is that faith is in the heart, while hope is in the mind. The second

WHEN FAITH CONTACTS GOD, IT IS
ALWAYS IN THE PRESENT.

difference between faith and hope is that faith is in the present, while hope is in the future. Faith is a substance, something that is already here. Hope is an expectation, something that of necessity looks toward the future.

In the years of my ministry, I cannot tell you how many people have come to me and said, "I have great faith; pray for me." I remember one man who said, "I have all the faith in the world." I thought, facetiously, that this was rather unfair because it left none for the rest of us! Seriously, every time I hear people say, "I have great faith," my heart sinks because my experience tells me they will not get what they claim to have faith for. They may be perfectly sincere, but their desires will go unanswered because they have confused faith with hope.

It is very easy to confuse faith and hope because, as we have already seen, hope is in the mind, while faith is in the heart. We usually know well enough what is in our minds, but it is much harder to know what is in our hearts. If a person has a strong expectation in his mind, he may mistakenly call it faith, but it is really hope. Lacking the necessary basis of faith, he does not see the results he expected.

There is an unpredictable quality about faith that mirrors the unpredictable nature of the human heart. Sometimes I have "felt" that I have had strong faith, but nothing has happened. At other times I have not "felt" any faith and yet have been pleasantly surprised at what God has done. The kind of faith that I can "feel" is usually mental—a substitute for the true heart faith. On the other hand, at times there can come forth out of my heart true, effective faith that I did not know was there, with results that amaze me!

Many people who say, "I believe that God will heal me," really mean, "I hope that He will heal me tomorrow." That is not faith, because faith is not for tomorrow; faith is something that we have now. If we keep directing our expectation toward the future, we are substituting hope for faith.

Years ago, when I was a student at Cambridge, the university gave me a grant to go to Athens for my studies in Greek antiquity. I soon lost interest in the statues and monuments of Greece and became much more interested in the people living in Greece. A friend from the university traveled with me, and every morning when we stepped outside our hotel, a group of shoeshine boys was waiting, determined to polish our shoes. If you have never traveled in a Mediterranean country, you have no idea how determined shoeshine boys can be. They will not take no for an answer. For the first two or three days, when we ventured outside our hotel, we tried saying, "*Ochi!*" throwing our heads backward with a scornful air at the same time. This is the Greek way of saying, "No!" But it simply did not work; the boys shined our shoes anyway.

About the fourth day, my friend tried a different tactic. When we stepped outside our hotel, the boys approached us to shine our shoes, as usual. This time my friend looked them squarely in the face and said, "*Avrio.*" They hesitated for a moment, and we were able to pass. Can you guess what *avrio* means? It means "tomorrow"!

Years later, after I had become a Christian, I recalled this incident. It illustrates so vividly the way the devil sometimes cheats Christians. When we are seeking healing for ourselves, or praying for the salvation of unsaved loved ones, the devil does not flatly say we will not obtain what we are seeking. He does not say, "You will not be healed," or "Your loved one will not be saved." If he did that, we would not listen to him. Instead, he says, "Yes, you will obtain what you are seeking, but not today; tomorrow!" And so we never come to the moment of obtaining what we are seeking. We are willing to accept the devil's "Tomorrow" when we would never accept his "No!" We have hope, but not faith.

However, God does not put us off until tomorrow. He says, "*Now is 'the acceptable time,' behold, now is 'the day of salvation'*" (2 Corinthians 6:2). God lives in the eternal *now*. To faith, He never reveals Himself as "I was," or as "I will be," but always as "I am." When faith contacts God, it is always in the present.

When we apply this principle to petitioning God, it will revolutionize this aspect of our prayer lives. In Mark 11:24, Jesus told us, *"Therefore I say to you, all things for which you pray and ask, believe that you have received them, and they shall be granted you."* When did Jesus tell us to receive what we pray for? At some undetermined point in the future? No, at the very moment we pray. We ask, and, at the same moment, we receive. Thereafter, we know that what we asked for will be granted to us.

Granting still remains in the future, but *receiving*, by faith, takes place when we pray. Having received now by faith, we know that, at God's appointed time, the things we received at the moment of praying will actually be granted to us. Faith to receive is in the present; the manifestation of what we have received is in the future. But without present faith, there is no assurance of future manifestation.

In Hebrews 4:3, the writer put the act of believing one stage further back in time than the act of receiving. He used the perfect tense: *"For we who have believed enter that rest."* Believing is here viewed as something already accomplished that does not need to be repeated. Having believed, we *"enter that rest."* There is no more struggle or anxiety. We know that what we have received by faith will in due course be manifested in experience. The receiving is our part of the transaction; the manifesting is God's.

SUMMARY

Faith and hope are closely related, yet there are two important differences between them. First, faith springs from the heart, but hope is entertained in the mind. Second, faith is in the present; it is a substance—something we already have. But hope is directed toward the future; it is an expectation of things to come.

Hopes that are based on true faith within the heart will not be disappointed. However, without this basis, there is no assurance that our hopes will be fulfilled.

Hope is God's appointed protection for our minds, but it will not obtain for us those results that God has promised only to faith. The key to obtaining what we ask from God is to receive it by faith at the very moment we petition Him. Doing this sets us free from continual struggle and anxiety, and brings us into an inner rest.

3

FAITH AS A GIFT

Faith, as depicted in the New Testament, has various aspects. Although its essential nature always agrees with the definition given in Hebrews 11:1, *"the substance of things hoped for, the evidence of things not seen"* (KJV), this nature expresses itself in a variety of distinct but related forms.

The three main forms of faith may be defined as follows:

1. Faith as a gift
2. Faith as a fruit
3. Faith to live by

The third form of faith is a continuing, personal relationship that links the believer directly to God and affects every area of his life. It provides the motivation, the direction, and the power for everything he does. It is, in fact, both the sole and the sufficient ground for righteous living. For this reason, I call it "faith to live by."

From chapter five onward in this book, we will thoroughly examine this form of faith. But first, in this chapter, we will examine the nature of faith as a gift. Then, in the next chapter, we will examine the nature of faith as a fruit.

"THE GIFTS OF THE SPIRIT ARE
TOOLS, NOT TOYS."
—BOB MUMFORD

THE NATURE OF SPIRITUAL GIFTS

In 1 Corinthians 12, Paul explained the gifts of the Holy Spirit. He opened the chapter with the statement, *"Now concerning spiritual gifts, brethren, I do not want you to be unaware"* (verse 1). Subsequently, he listed nine distinct gifts:

> *But to each one is given the manifestation of the Spirit for the common good. For to one is given the word of wisdom through the Spirit, and to another the word of knowledge according to the same Spirit; to another faith by the same Spirit, and to another gifts of healing by the one Spirit, and to another the effecting of miracles, and to another prophecy, and to another the distinguishing of spirits, to another various kinds of tongues, and to another the interpretation of tongues. But one and the same Spirit works all these things, distributing to each one individually just as He wills.*
>
> (1 Corinthians 12:7–11)

The key word that explains the distinctive nature of these gifts is *"manifestation"* (verse 7). The Holy Spirit Himself, dwelling in a believer, is invisible. But by these gifts operating through a believer, the presence of the Holy Spirit is made manifest to human senses. In each case, the results produced are in the realm of the senses; they can be seen or heard or felt.

Since these gifts are not manifestations of the believer's own personality but of the person of the Holy Spirit within the believer, all of them are supernatural in character. In every case, the results they produce are on a higher level than the believer could ever achieve by his ability alone. Each result is possible only through a direct, supernatural operation of the Holy Spirit. By these gifts, and through the believer, the Holy Spirit comes forth out of the invisible spiritual realm and makes a direct impact upon the physical world of space and time.

FAITH HAS ITS
ORIGIN IN GOD—NOT MAN.

Paul established two important practical points concerning these gifts. First, they are distributed solely at the discretion of the Holy Spirit, according to His sovereign purposes for each believer's ministry. Human will or achievement is not the basis for receiving these spiritual gifts. Second, they are given *"to each one… for the common good"* (1 Corinthians 12:7), for a useful, practical purpose. As Bible teacher Bob Mumford said, "The gifts of the Spirit are tools, not toys."

It has often been pointed out that these nine gifts fall naturally into three groups of three:

1. *The gifts of utterance.* These are gifts that operate through the believer's vocal organs. They include prophecy, kinds of tongues, and the interpretation of tongues.

2. *The gifts of revelation.* These are gifts that impart spiritual illumination. They include a word of wisdom, a word of knowledge, and the distinguishing of spirits (or discernings of spirits).

3. *The gifts of power.* These are gifts that demonstrate God's supernatural power in the physical realm. They include faith, gifts of healings, and workings of miracles.

HAVE GOD'S FAITH

The gift of faith, which we will now study, is the first of the three gifts of power. It is distinguished from the other forms of faith by the fact that it is a sovereign, supernatural manifestation of the Holy Spirit working through the believer. The two key words are *sovereign* and *supernatural*.

In Matthew 21 and Mark 11, we read that Jesus, on His way to Jerusalem with His disciples, came to a fig tree by the side of the road. Jesus was seeking fruit. When He found that the tree contained only leaves, but no fruit, He pronounced a curse upon it, saying, *"May no one ever eat fruit from you again!"* (Mark 11:14).

THE HOLY SPIRIT IMPARTS A
PORTION OF GOD'S OWN DIVINE
FAITH TO THE BELIEVER.

The next day, as Jesus and His disciples passed the same tree, the disciples were astonished to see that, within twenty-four hours, it had withered from the roots up. *"Rabbi, behold,"* Peter commented, *"the fig tree which You cursed has withered"* (verse 21).

To Peter's comment, Jesus replied, *"Have faith in God"* (verse 22). This is how His answer has been translated into English. However, what Jesus actually said, in its most literal form, was, "Have God's faith." This statement highlights the special kind of faith we are speaking of here, that is, faith as a gift. Faith has its origin not in man, but in God. It is an aspect of God's own eternal nature. Through the gift of faith, the Holy Spirit imparts a portion of God's own faith, directly and supernaturally, to the believer. This is faith on a divine level, as high above mere human faith as heaven is above earth.

In saying, "Have God's faith," Jesus challenged His disciples to receive and exercise this kind of faith, just as He Himself had done. He went on to tell them that with faith of this kind, they would not only be able to do what they had seen Him do to the fig tree, but they would also be able to move a mountain by simply speaking:

> *Truly I say to you, if you have faith, and do not doubt, you shall not only do what was done to the fig tree, but even if you say to this mountain, "Be taken up and cast into the sea," it shall happen.* (Matthew 21:21)

Jesus was not speaking merely to the disciples when He said, *"If you have faith,"* for we see in Mark 11:23 that He used the word *whoever,* extending His promise to all believers:

> *Truly I say to you, whoever says to this mountain, "Be taken up and cast into the sea," and does not doubt in his heart, but believes that what he says is going to happen, it shall be granted him.*

IT IS NOT THE *QUANTITY*
OF THE FAITH THAT MATTERS,
BUT THE *QUALITY*.

Jesus set no limit to the scope of this kind of faith. The phrases He used are all-inclusive: *"Whoever says…what he says…shall be granted him."* There is no restriction concerning the person who speaks or the words that are spoken. All that matters is the nature of the faith; it must be God's own faith.

In Luke 8:22–25, we see that as Jesus and His disciples were crossing the Sea of Galilee in a boat, they were suddenly overtaken by an unnaturally violent storm. The disciples woke Jesus, who was asleep in the stern, saying, *"Master, Master, we are perishing!"* (verse 24). The biblical record continues, *"And being aroused, He rebuked the wind and the surging waves, and they stopped, and it became calm"* (verse 24).

Obviously, the faith that Jesus exercised here was not on the human level. Normally, the winds and the waters are not under man's control. But at the moment of need, Jesus received a special impartation of His Father's own faith. Then, by a word spoken with that faith, He accomplished what man would consider impossible: the instantaneous calming of the storm.

When the danger had passed, Jesus turned to His disciples and said, *"Where is **your** faith?"* (verse 25). In other words, He asked, "Why couldn't *you* have done that? Why did *I* have to do it?" He implied that it would have been just as easy for the disciples to have calmed the storm as it had been for Him—if they had exercised the right kind of faith. But in the moment of crisis, the impact of the storm on the disciples' senses had opened the way for fear to enter their hearts, thus excluding faith. Jesus, on the other hand, had opened His heart to the Father and had received from Him the supernatural gift of faith needed to deal with the storm.

QUALITY, NOT QUANTITY

Later, Jesus confronted a storm of a different kind: a boy rolling on the ground in an epileptic seizure and his agonized father

WHEN A BELIEVER OPERATES IN
DIVINE FAITH, HIS WORDS ARE AS
EFFECTIVE AS IF GOD HIMSELF
HAD SPOKEN THEM.

imploring help. Jesus dealt with this storm as He had dealt with the one on the Sea of Galilee. He spoke an authoritative word of faith, which drove the evil spirit out of the boy. When His disciples asked Him why they had not been able to do this, He told them plainly, *"Because of the littleness of your faith"* (Matthew 17:20). Then He went on to say, *"If you have faith as a mustard seed, you shall say to this mountain, 'Move from here to there,' and it shall move; and nothing shall be impossible to you"* (verse 20).

Here Jesus used a mustard seed as a measure of quantity. In Matthew 13:32, we are told that a mustard seed is *"smaller than all other seeds."* In other words, Jesus was telling us that it is not the *quantity* of the faith that matters, but the *quality*. If a person has the right kind of faith in even the amount of a mustard seed, it is sufficient to move a mountain!

Near the climax of His earthly ministry, Jesus once more demonstrated the power of words spoken with the right kind of faith. Outside the tomb of Lazarus, *"He cried out with a loud voice, 'Lazarus, come forth'"* (John 11:43). This brief command, energized by supernatural faith, caused a man who was both dead and buried to come walking out of his tomb, alive and well.

The original pattern for supernatural faith is found in the act of creation itself. It was by faith in His own word that God brought the universe into being. *"By the word of the LORD the heavens were made, and by the breath [literally, spirit] of His mouth all their host.... For He spoke, and it was done; He commanded, and it stood fast"* (Psalm 33:6, 9). God's spoken word, energized by His Spirit, was the effective agent in all creation.

When the gift of faith is in operation, a person becomes, for a time, the channel of God's own faith. The one who speaks is no longer important, but only the faith that is expressed. If it is God's own faith at work, it is equally effective whether the words are spoken through God's mouth or whether they are uttered by the Holy Spirit through the mouth of a human believer. As long

PRAYER PRAYED WITH GOD-GIVEN
FAITH IS IRRESISTIBLE.

as a believer operates with this divine faith, his words are just as effective as if God Himself had spoken them. It is the faith that matters, not the person.

In the examples we have considered up to this point, this supernatural faith was expressed through a spoken word. By a spoken word, Jesus caused the fig tree to wither. By a spoken word, He calmed the storm, cast the evil spirit out of the epileptic boy, and called Lazarus out of the tomb. In Mark 11:23, Jesus said this about any word spoken in faith: *"Whoever says…what he says… shall be granted him."*

Sometimes a word spoken in prayer becomes the channel for the gift of faith. In James 5:15, we are told that *"the prayer of faith shall save* [or, restore] *the sick"* (KJV). There is no room left for doubt about the effect of a prayer of faith. Its results are guaranteed. Prayer prayed with God-given faith is irresistible. Neither sickness nor any other condition that is contrary to God's will can stand against it.

James referred to Elijah as an example of someone who prayed *"the prayer of faith."* By his prayer, Elijah withheld all rain for three and a half years, and then caused rain to fall again. (See James 5:17–18.) Scripture indicates that the giving and withholding of rain is a divine prerogative, exercised by God Himself. (See, for example, Deuteronomy 11:13–17; Jeremiah 5:24; 14:22.) Yet, for three and a half years, Elijah exercised this prerogative on God's behalf. James emphasized that *"Elijah was a man with a nature like ours"* (James 5:17)—a human being just like the rest of us. But as long as he was enabled to pray with God's faith, the words he uttered were as effective as God's own decrees.

However, faith of this kind does not need to operate through a spoken word only. It was by this same kind of supernatural faith that Jesus was able to walk on the stormy Sea of Galilee. (See Matthew 14:25–33.) In this case, He did not need to speak; He merely walked out onto the water. Peter began to follow the

GOD-GIVEN FAITH MEETS A
SPECIFIC NEED AND REMAINS
UNDER HIS CONTROL.

example of Jesus, exercising the same kind of faith. This enabled him to do precisely the same thing that Jesus was doing. But when he looked away from Jesus to the waves, his faith deserted him, and he began to sink!

The comment that Jesus made is very illuminating: *"O you of little faith, why did you doubt?"* (Matthew 14:31). Jesus did not reprove Peter for wanting to walk on the water. He reproved him for losing faith in the middle of doing so. Don Basham, the author of several books on the power of the Holy Spirit, has pointed out that there is a divine urge implanted in every human heart to step out in supernatural faith and to walk on a plane above the level of our own ability. Since God Himself placed this urge in man, He does not reprove us for it. On the contrary, He is willing to give us the faith that will enable us to do these things. He is not disappointed when we reach out for this kind of faith, but only when we do not hold on to it long enough.

GOD RETAINS THE INITIATIVE

This supernatural kind of faith is given in a specific situation to meet a specific need. It remains under God's direct control. It must remain so, for it is God's own faith. He gives it or withholds it at His discretion. This type of faith is included with all the other supernatural gifts, concerning which Paul said, *"But one and the same Spirit works all these things, distributing to each one individually just as He wills"* (1 Corinthians 12:11). The key phrase here is at the end—*"just as He wills."* God Himself determines when and to whom He will impart each of the spiritual gifts. The initiative is with God, not with man.

This was true even in the ministry of Jesus Himself. He did not curse every fruitless fig tree. He did not calm every storm. He did not call every dead man out of his tomb. He did not always walk on the water. He was careful to leave the initiative in the hands of His Father. In John 5:19, He said, *"The Son can do nothing of*

THE GIFT OF FAITH CAN BE A
CATALYST FOR THE GIFTS OF
HEALINGS AND MIRACLES.

Himself, unless it is something He sees the Father doing; for whatever the Father does, these things the Son also does in like manner." Again, Jesus said in John 14:10, *"The words that I say to you I do not speak on My own initiative, but the Father abiding in Me does His works."* The initiative was always with the Father.

We must learn to be as reverent and as careful in our relationship with the Father as Jesus was. The gift of faith is not ours to command. It is not intended to satisfy our personal whims or ambitions. It is made available at God's discretion to accomplish ends that originate in God's own eternal purposes. We cannot, and must not, wrest the initiative from God. Even if God would permit us to do so, it would ultimately be to our own loss.

Pictured as a mustard seed, the gift of faith is similar to two of the gifts of revelation: a word of wisdom, which is directive, and a word of knowledge, which is informative. God has all wisdom and all knowledge, but, fortunately for us, He does not burden us with all of it. However, in a given situation in which we need direction, He supernaturally imparts to us a word of wisdom—just one little "mustard seed" out of His total store of wisdom. Or, in a situation in which we need information, He imparts to us a word of knowledge—a little "mustard seed" out of His total store of knowledge.

So it is with the gift of faith. God has all faith, but He does not impart it all to us. In a given situation in which we need faith on a higher level than our own, God imparts to us a "mustard seed" of faith out of His own total store. Once the special need has been met, God withdraws His faith, and we are left once again to exercise our own.

EQUIPMENT FOR EVANGELISM

As we saw earlier, the gift of faith is associated with the other two gifts of power: gifts of healings and workings of miracles. In practice, the gift of faith often serves as a catalyst to bring the other two gifts into operation. This is illustrated by the ministry of Philip in Samaria, as described in the book of Acts:

> *And Philip went down to the city of Samaria and began pro-claiming Christ to them. And the multitudes with one accord were giving attention to what was said by Philip, as they heard and saw the signs which he was performing. For in the case of many who had unclean spirits, they were coming out of them shouting with a loud voice; and many who had been paralyzed and lame were healed. And there was much rejoicing in that city.* (Acts 8:5–8)

In the first phase of his ministry, Philip cast out evil spirits. As we have seen from the example of Jesus, as recorded in Matthew 17:14–21 and elsewhere, evil spirits were cast out by the spoken word through the exercise of the gift of faith. In the second phase of Philip's ministry, the other two gifts of power, miracles and healings, came into operation. As a result, miracles were performed and the paralyzed and the lame were healed.

In Acts 21:8, Philip is called *"the evangelist."* Only two patterns of the ministry of an evangelist are presented to us in the New Testament: that of Jesus Himself and that of Philip. In each case, there was a strong emphasis on the casting out of evil spirits, which was followed by miracles and healings. The three gifts of power—faith, miracles, and healings—together constitute the supernatural equipment that is endorsed by the New Testament for the ministry of an evangelist.

SUMMARY

The gift of faith is one of nine gifts of the Holy Spirit listed by Paul in 1 Corinthians 12:7–11. Each of these gifts is a supernatural manifestation of the Holy Spirit, who dwells in believers and operates through them.

Through the gift of faith, the Holy Spirit temporarily imparts to a believer a portion of God's own faith. This is faith on a divine level, far above the human level. It is not the quantity that matters, but the quality. A "mustard seed" of this kind of faith is sufficient to move a mountain.

The gift of faith operates frequently, but not exclusively, through a spoken word. Such a word may be spoken in prayer. Through this gift, Jesus caused a fig tree to wither, calmed a storm at sea, drove an evil spirit out of an epileptic boy, called Lazarus out of his tomb, and walked on the stormy waves.

God has implanted in man an urge to exercise this kind of faith. Therefore, He does not reprove us for doing so. Rather, He is disappointed if we let go of it too soon. However, as in the ministry of Jesus, the initiative must always be left with God.

The gift of faith can serve as a catalyst for the related gifts of healings and miracles. These three gifts combined are the equipment endorsed by the New Testament for the ministry of an evangelist.

SPIRITUAL FRUIT EXPRESSES
THE NATURE OF THE LIFE
IT COMES FROM.

4

FAITH AS A FRUIT

In the preceding chapter, we looked at how faith operates as one of the nine spiritual gifts listed by Paul in 1 Corinthians 12:7–11. In this chapter, we will explore how faith functions as one of the nine forms of spiritual fruit that Paul listed in Galatians 5:22–23: *"But the fruit of the Spirit is love, joy, peace, longsuffering, gentleness, goodness, faith, meekness, temperance"* (kjv).

The seventh form of fruit listed is faith. Recent versions of the Bible offer a variety of translations for this word, such as "faithfulness," "fidelity," and "trustfulness." However, the Greek noun that Paul used here is *pistis*. As we saw in chapter one, this is the basic word used for faith throughout the New Testament.

GIFTS VERSUS FRUIT

Before we begin to study this particular form of fruit, it will be helpful to consider the relationship between gifts and fruit in general. What is the difference?

One way to bring the difference into focus is to picture a Christmas tree and an apple tree side by side. I am talking about a Christmas tree on which presents are tied. It is a common practice in some places to tie gifts onto the Christmas tree, instead of

GIFTS EXPRESS *ABILITY*, WHILE
FRUIT EXPRESSES *CHARACTER*.

placing them under the tree. In this way, a Christmas tree "bears" gifts, while an apple tree bears fruit.

In the case of the Christmas tree, a gift is both attached to it and removed from it by a single, brief act. The gift may be a garment, and the tree may be a fir tree. There is no direct connection between the tree and the gift. The gift tells us nothing about the nature of the tree from which it is taken.

On the other hand, there is a direct connection between an apple and the tree that bears it. The nature of the tree determines the nature of the fruit, both its kind and its quality. An apple tree can never bear an orange. A healthy tree will bear healthy fruit; an unhealthy tree will bear unhealthy fruit. (See, for example, Matthew 7:17–20.) The fruit on the apple tree is not produced by a single act; rather, it is the result of a steady, continuing process of growth and development. To produce the best fruit, the tree must be carefully cultivated. This requires time, skill, and labor.

Let us apply this simple analogy to the spiritual realm. A spiritual gift is both imparted and received by a single, brief transaction. It tells us nothing about the nature of the person who exercises it. On the other hand, spiritual fruit expresses the nature of the life from which it proceeds; it comes only as the result of a process of growth. To attain the best fruit, a life must be carefully cultivated through time, skill, and labor.

I may describe the difference in another way by saying that gifts express *ability*, while fruit expresses *character*. Which is more important? In the long run, character is undoubtedly more important than ability. The exercise of gifts is temporary. As Paul explained in 1 Corinthians 13:8–13, there will come a time when gifts will no longer be needed. But character is permanent. The character that we develop in this life will determine what we will be throughout eternity. We will one day leave our gifts behind; our character will be with us forever.

FAITH IS A QUIET, STEADY TRUST
IN THE GOODNESS, WISDOM, AND
FAITHFULNESS OF GOD.

However, we do not need to choose one at the expense of the other. Gifts do not exclude fruit; fruit does not exclude gifts. Rather, they are intended to complement each other. Gifts should provide practical expression for character, just as they did perfectly in the person of Jesus Himself. His loving, gracious character was expressed by the fullest possible exercise of spiritual gifts. Only through the gifts could He meet the needs of the people to whom He had come to minister, fully expressing to them the nature of His heavenly Father, whom He had come to represent. (See, for example, John 14:9–10.)

We should seek to follow Christ's pattern. The more we develop the attributes that characterized Jesus—love, concern, and compassion—the more we will need the same gifts that He exercised in order to give practical expression to these attributes. The more fully we are equipped with these gifts, the greater our ability will be to glorify God our Father, just as Jesus did.

Fruit, then, is an expression of character. When all nine forms of spiritual fruit are present and fully developed, they represent the totality of Christian character, each form of fruit satisfying a specific need and each complementing the rest. Within this totality, the fruit of faith may be viewed from two aspects. These two aspects correspond to two different but related uses of the Greek word *pistis*. The first is trust; the second is trustworthiness.

FAITH AS TRUST

The first aspect of faith as a fruit is trust. The *Jerusalem Bible* translates *pistis* as *"trustfulness."* Over and over again, Jesus emphasized that one of the requirements for all who would enter the kingdom of God is to become like a little child. (See Matthew 18:1–3; 19:13–14; Mark 10:13–15; Luke 18:15–17.) There is probably no quality more distinctively characteristic of childhood than trustfulness. And yet, paradoxically, it is a quality that is seen at its perfection in the most mature men of God—men such as

THE KEY TO COMPLETE TRUST IN
GOD IS COMMITMENT.

Abraham, Moses, David, and Paul. We may conclude, therefore, that the degree to which we cultivate trustfulness is a good measure of our spiritual maturity.

More fully, the fruit of faith—in this aspect of trustfulness—may be defined as a quiet, steady, unwavering trust in the goodness, wisdom, and faithfulness of God. No matter what trials or seeming disasters may be encountered, the person who has cultivated this form of fruit remains calm and restful in the midst of them all. He has an unshakable confidence that God is still in complete control of every situation and that, in and through all circumstances, God is working out His own purpose of blessing for each one of His children.

The outward expression of this kind of trust is stability. This is beautifully pictured by David in Psalm 125:1: *"Those who trust in the LORD are as Mount Zion, which cannot be moved, but abides forever."* All earth's mountains may tremble and shake and even be totally removed—except one. Zion can never be moved. God has chosen it for His own dwelling place, and it alone will abide forever.

So it is with the believer who has learned to trust. Others all around him may give way to panic and confusion, but he remains calm and secure. *"His foundation is in the holy mountains"* (Psalm 87:1).

About 1960, while I was serving as the principal of a training college for African teachers in western Kenya, one of our women students, named Agneta, contracted typhoid. My wife and I visited her in the hospital and found her critically ill. She was in a deep coma. I prayed that God would bring her out of the coma long enough for me to speak to her. A moment later, she opened her eyes and looked up at me.

"Agneta," I said, "do you know for sure that your soul is safe in the Lord's hands?"

"Yes," she said in a clear, firm voice—and then immediately lapsed into a coma again. But I was satisfied. That one word, *yes*, was all she needed to say and all I needed to hear. It expressed a deep, untroubled trust that nothing in this world could shake or overthrow.

The key to this kind of trust is commitment. About a year previously, in my presence, Agneta had made a definite, personal commitment of her life to Jesus Christ. Now, in the hour of testing—perhaps at the very threshold of eternity—she did not need to make any further commitment. She needed only to rest in the commitment she had already made—one that included both life and death, both time and eternity.

In His timing, God answered the prayers of Agneta's fellow students and raised her up again to full health. Her ability to receive the influence of the prayers offered on her behalf was in large measure due to her attitude of trust.

In Psalm 37:5, David said, "*Commit your way to the* Lord, *trust also in Him, and He will do it.*" More literally, the verse says, "And He is doing it." Two things are here required of us. The first is an act: "*commit.*" The second is an attitude: "*trust.*" The act of commitment leads to the attitude of trust. David assured us that, as long as we continue in this attitude of trust, God "is doing it." In other words, God is working out what we have committed to Him. It is the continuing attitude of trust on our part that keeps the channel open through which God is able to intervene in our lives and work out what needs to be done. But if we abandon our trust, we close off the channel and hinder the completion of what God has begun to do for us.

Committing a matter to the Lord is like taking cash to the bank and depositing it into your account. Once you have received the teller's receipt for your deposit, you no longer need to be concerned about the safety of your money. That is now the bank's responsibility, not yours. It is ironic that some people who have no difficulty in trusting a bank to take care of the money they have deposited find it much harder to trust God concerning some vital, personal matter they have committed to Him.

The example of the bank deposit illustrates one important factor in making a successful commitment. When you walk out of the bank, you carry an official receipt, indicating the date, the place, and the amount of your deposit. There are no uncertainties. In the same way, you need to be equally specific concerning those things that you commit to God. You need to know, without a shadow of a doubt, both *what* you have committed and *when* and *where* the commitment was made. You also need the Holy Spirit's official "receipt," acknowledging that God has accepted your commitment. (See, for example, Romans 15:13.)

TRUST MUST BE CULTIVATED

Trust is like all forms of fruit: it needs to be cultivated, and it passes through various stages of development before it reaches full maturity. The development of trust is well illustrated by the words of David in Psalm 62. In verse two, he said, *"He [God] only is my rock and my salvation, my stronghold; I shall not be greatly shaken."* But in verse six, after making exactly the same declaration of trust in God, he said, *"I shall not be shaken."* Between verse two and verse six, David progressed from not being *"greatly shaken"* to not being *"shaken"* at all.

We need to be as honest about ourselves as David was. Before our trust has come to maturity, the best that we can say is, "I will not be greatly shaken!" At this stage, troubles and opposition will shake us, but they will not overthrow us. However, if we continue to cultivate our trust, we will come to the stage where we can say, "I will not be shaken at all!" Nothing will be able to shake us any longer—much less overthrow us.

Trust of this kind is in the realm of the spirit rather than the emotions. We may turn once more to the personal testimony

GOD HIMSELF IS BOTH
THE BEGINNING AND THE
END OF FAITH.

of David for an illustration. In Psalm 56:3, he said to the Lord, *"When I am afraid, I will put my trust in Thee."* Here David recognized two conflicting influences at work in himself simultaneously: fear and trust. However, fear is superficial, in the emotions; trust is deeper down, in the spirit.

Mature trust is like a deep, strong river relentlessly making its way to the sea. At times, the winds of fear or doubt may blow contrary to the river's course and whip up foaming waves on its surface. But these winds and waves cannot change or hinder the deep, continuing flow of the waters below the surface. They follow the path marked out for them by the riverbed to their predetermined destination in the sea.

Trust, in its full maturity, is beautifully depicted by the following words of Paul:

> *For this reason I also suffer these things, but I am not ashamed;*
> *for I know whom I have believed and I am convinced that He is*
> *able to guard what I have entrusted to Him until that day.*
> (2 Timothy 1:12)

By all worldly standards, Paul at this stage was a failure. Some of his most influential friends and supporters had turned against him. Of all his close coworkers, only Luke remained with him. One of his coworkers, Demas, had actually abandoned him and turned back to the world. Paul was weak and aged, a chained prisoner in a Roman jail, awaiting unjust trial and execution at the hands of a cruel, depraved despot. Yet his words ring with serene, unshakable confidence: *"I am not ashamed...I know...I have believed...I am convinced."* Beyond the horizon of time, he looked forward to an unclouded day—*"that day"*—the day when another judge, the righteous Judge, would award him *"the crown of righteousness"* (2 Timothy 4:8).

As it was with David, so it was with Paul: trust was the outcome of an act of commitment. His commitment is expressed in his own words: *"He is able to guard what I have entrusted to Him"* (2 Timothy 1:12). *Trusting* was the result of *entrusting.* Years previously, Paul had made an irrevocable commitment of himself to Christ. Out of this, subsequent trials and sufferings gradually brought forth an ever deepening trust that had now come to its full fruition in a Roman dungeon, its radiance all the brighter in contrast to its gloomy setting.

FAITH AS TRUSTWORTHINESS

Now we will examine the second aspect of faith as a fruit: trustworthiness. Linguistically, "trustworthiness" is, in fact, the original meaning of *pistis.* In Arndt and Gingrich's standard lexicon of New Testament Greek, the first specific definition of *pistis* is "faithfulness, reliability." If we go back to the Old Testament, the same meaning applies to the Hebrew word for faith—*emunah.* Its primary meaning is "faithfulness"; its secondary meaning is "faith." The verb from which it is derived gives us the word *amen*— "so be it," "let it be confirmed." The root meaning is "firm, reliable."

Both meanings alike—trust and trustworthiness—converge in the person and nature of God Himself. If we view faith as trust, its only ultimate basis is God's trustworthiness. If we view faith as trustworthiness, it is only through our trust that the Holy Spirit is able to impart to us God's trustworthiness. God Himself is both the beginning and the end of faith. His trustworthiness is the only basis for our trust; our trust in Him reproduces His trustworthiness in us.

Probably no attribute of God is more persistently emphasized throughout the Scriptures than His trustworthiness. In the Old Testament, there is one special Hebrew word reserved for the attribute: *chesed.* In the English versions of the Bible, this word is variously translated "goodness," "kindness," "lovingkindness," "mercy," and so on. However, not one of these translations fully expresses its meaning.

There are two distinctive features of God's *chesed*, or trustworthiness. First, it is the expression of God's free, unmerited grace. It goes beyond anything that man can ever deserve or demand as a right. Second, it is always based on a covenant that God voluntarily enters into. We may combine these two features by saying that *chesed* is God's trustworthiness in fulfilling His covenant commitments, which go beyond anything that we can deserve or demand.

Thus, we find a close connection between the following three important Hebrew concepts: *emunah*, faith or faithfulness; *chesed*, God's trustworthiness; and *berith*, which means "a covenant." These three Hebrew words form a recurrent theme in a series of verses in Psalm 89:

> *And My faithfulness [emunah] and My lovingkindness [chesed] will be with him.*   (verse 24)

> *My lovingkindness [chesed] I will keep for him forever, and My covenant [berith] shall be confirmed [aman, or amen] to him.*   (verse 28)

> *But I will not break off My lovingkindness [chesed] from him, nor deal falsely in My faithfulness [emunah]. My covenant [berith] I will not violate, nor will I alter the utterance of My lips.*   (verses 33–34)

Verse 34 brings out a special relationship between God's trustworthiness and the words of His mouth. There are two things God will never do: break His covenant or go back on what He has said. God's trustworthiness, imparted by the Holy Spirit, will reproduce the same characteristic in us. It will make us people of unfailing integrity and honesty.

In Psalm 15:1, David asked two questions: "O LORD, who may abide in Thy tent? Who may dwell on Thy holy hill?" In the verses that follow, he answered his own questions by listing eleven

GOD EXPECTS BELIEVERS TO BE
TRUE TO THEIR COMMITMENTS,
EVEN AT THE COST
OF PERSONAL SACRIFICE.

characteristics that mark a person of integrity. The ninth requirement is listed at the end of verse four: *"He swears to his own hurt,
and does not change."* God expects the believer to be true to his
commitments, even at the cost of personal sacrifice. The world
has its own way of saying this: "A man is as good as his word."
A Christian who does not honor his word and keep his commitments has not yet developed the fruit of trustworthiness.

While God requires this kind of trustworthiness in our dealings with all men, we have a special obligation toward our fellow
Christians. God's own trustworthiness (*chesed*) is based, as we
have seen, on His covenant (*berith*). Through Jesus Christ, He has
brought us into a covenant relationship both with Himself and
with other believers. The distinguishing mark of this relationship
is that we exhibit, both toward God and toward our fellow believers, the same trustworthiness that God has so richly and freely
demonstrated toward us.

We have already seen that God's *chesed*, expressed in His covenant commitments, is based on His grace, going beyond anything
that we, who are its recipients, can ever deserve or demand. This
grace, too, will be reflected in our covenant relationships with our
fellow believers. We will not limit ourselves to the mere requirements of justice or of some legal form of contract. We will be ready
to make the full commitment that God made in establishing His
covenant with us: to lay down our lives for one another. *"We know
love by this, that He laid down His life for us; and we ought to lay
down our lives for the brethren"* (1 John 3:16). It is by the laying
down of our lives that we enter into full covenant relationship with
God and with one another.

Scripture paints a fearful picture of the breakdown of moral
and ethical standards that will mark the close of the present age:

> *You must face the fact: the final age of this world is to be a
> time of troubles. Men will love nothing but money and self;*

they will be arrogant, boastful, and abusive; with no respect for parents, no gratitude, no piety, no natural affection; they will be implacable in their hatreds, scandal-mongers, intemperate and fierce, strangers to all goodness, traitors, adventurers, swollen with self-importance. They will be men who put pleasure in the place of God, men who preserve the outward form of religion, but are a standing denial of its reality. Keep clear of men like these. (2 Timothy 3:1–5 NEB)

The Greek word that is here translated as *"implacable in their hatreds"* is defined in Thayer's lexicon as denoting "those who cannot be persuaded to enter into a covenant." The whole trend of this world will be—indeed, already is—away from those moral and ethical characteristics that a covenant demands. As the world thus plunges deeper into darkness, God's people must, by contrast, be more determined than ever to walk in the light of fellowship. We must show ourselves both willing and qualified to enter into and maintain those covenant relationships on which fellowship depends.

For this purpose, we will need to cultivate the fruit of trustworthiness to full maturity.

SUMMARY

Spiritual fruit differs from spiritual gifts in two main ways. First, a spiritual gift can be both imparted and received by a single, brief transaction; fruit must be cultivated by a continuing process that requires time, skill, and labor. Second, gifts are not directly related to the character of those who exercise them; fruit is an expression of character. Ideally, fruit and gifts should balance one another in a combination that glorifies God and serves humanity.

As a form of fruit, faith may be understood in two distinct but related ways: as trust and as trustworthiness.

Stability is a manifestation of trust, and it increases as trust matures. Stability requires an initial act of commitment. Entrusting leads to trusting.

Our trust is based on God's trustworthiness, or *chesed*. God demonstrates His trustworthiness toward us by fulfilling His covenant commitments, which go beyond anything we can deserve or demand. In turn, God's trustworthiness makes us the kind of people who are willing and able to enter into and maintain covenant commitments, both with God and with one another.

A LIFE OF RIGHTEOUSNESS HAS ITS
SOURCE IN GOD ALONE.

5

FAITH TO LIVE BY

About six centuries before the Christian era, God gave the prophet Habakkuk a revelation that was to provide the basis of the gospel: *"But the righteous will live by his faith"* (Habakkuk 2:4). So accurately does this prophecy express the central theme of the Christian message that it is actually quoted three times in the New Testament: in Romans 1:17, in Galatians 3:11, and in Hebrews 10:38.

ONLY ONE BASIS: FAITH

Of the above three passages, Habakkuk's prophecy is most fully expounded in Romans. In fact, it provides the central theme for the entire epistle. To obtain a proper perspective on the book of Romans as a whole, we may compare the epistle to a symphony by a great composer such as Beethoven. The first fifteen verses of chapter one are the introduction. Then, in verses sixteen and seventeen, Paul presented the main theme: *"The righteous man shall live by faith"* (verse 17).

The symphony is then divided into three main movements. The first consists of chapters one through eight. In this movement, Paul's approach was doctrinal. He worked out a detailed, logical analysis of his theme, showing how it harmonizes with the

LIFE IN CHRIST IS
A PRESENT REALITY, NOT JUST
A FUTURE HOPE.

prophecies and the patterns of the Old Testament. The second movement consists of chapters nine, ten, and eleven. Here Paul applied his theme to Israel. He showed how Israel's attempt to achieve righteousness by works rather than by faith had blinded them to their Messiah, thus depriving them of the blessings offered to them by God through Christ. The third movement consists of chapters twelve through sixteen. Here Paul emphasized the practical. He showed how his theme must be worked out in various activities, relationships, and duties of daily living.

To appreciate a symphony properly, we need to pick out the composer's main theme when it is first introduced and then follow it carefully through the whole piece. Unless we keep the main theme in mind, we will not fully appreciate the various modifications and developments it undergoes in the successive movements. The same principle applies to the book of Romans. First of all, we need to grasp the main theme that runs throughout the whole epistle, which we have established as *"the righteous man shall live by faith"* (Romans 1:17). Then we need to keep this theme always in mind as we study the epistle's main divisions, noting how it applies to each particular subject that is dealt with. This will give unity and consistency to our understanding of the whole book.

In Romans 1:16, Paul stated the one basic requirement for experiencing the power of God for salvation: *"For I am not ashamed of the gospel, for it is the power of God for salvation to everyone who believes, to the Jew first and also to the Greek."*

Salvation is made available to *"everyone who believes, to the Jew first and also to the Greek."* There are no exceptions. Differences of religious or racial background are irrelevant. In God's all-inclusive offer of salvation to the human race, He has laid down one simple requirement that never varies. It is *faith.*

In verse seventeen, Paul went on to explain how this truth of salvation can be known: *"For in it* [the gospel] *the righteousness of God is revealed from faith to faith; as it is written, 'But the righteous man shall live by faith.'"* The word *faith* occurs three times in this verse. God's revelation comes *from* faith *to* faith. It originates in God's own faith—faith that His word will accomplish its preordained purpose. It is transmitted through the faith of the one who delivers the message. It is appropriated by the faith of the one who receives the message. From beginning to end, the theme is faith.

Let us examine the message more closely. It could not be stated more simply: *"The righteous man shall live by faith."* Obviously, in this context, "to live" means more than to have normal, physical life. We know that even the wicked and the ungodly have that kind of life. But Scripture reveals that there is another kind of life—a life of righteousness—that has its source in God alone. The only way anyone can receive this kind of life is by faith in Jesus Christ.

In his gospel, the apostle John continually focused on this divine, eternal life. At the opening, in John 1:4, he told us concerning Jesus, *"In Him was life."* In John 3:36, he recorded John the Baptist's testimony concerning Jesus: *"He who believes in the Son has eternal life."* In John 6:47, Jesus Himself said, *"He who believes has eternal life."* Again, John 10:10 says, *"I came that they might have life, and might have it abundantly."* And John 10:27–28 states, *"My sheep hear My voice, and I know them, and they follow Me; and I give eternal life to them."* Finally, near the close of his gospel, John stated the main purpose for which it was written: *"That you may believe that Jesus is the Christ, the Son of God; and that believing you may have life in His name"* (John 20:31).

In his first epistle, John returned to this theme:

> *And the witness is this, that God has given us eternal life, and this life is in His Son. He who has the Son has the life; he who does not have the Son of God does not have the life. These things I have written to you who believe in the name of the Son of God, in order that you may know that you have eternal life.* (1 John 5:11–13)

It is important to see that John used the present tense throughout. *"He who has the Son **has** the life." "You who believe…**have** eternal life."*

Paul also spoke of this life in Christ in brief and vivid phrases. In Philippians 1:21, he said, *"For to me, to live is Christ."* And in Colossians 3:4, he said, *"Christ…is our life."* For Paul, as it was for John, life in Christ was a present reality, not just a future hope.

This, then, is the essence of the gospel message. There is a divine, eternal life that has its source in God alone. God has made this life available to us in Jesus Christ. As we receive Jesus by faith into our hearts and yield our lives to Him in full obedience, we receive in Him the very life of God Himself. This life is not something reserved for another world or a future existence. It is something that we can experience here and now. *"He who has the Son has the life"* (1 John 5:12). We have everlasting life at this very moment—and on into eternity. It is ours to enjoy from the very moment that we truly put our faith in Jesus Christ.

Having thus received this new kind of life through faith in Christ, we are faced with the challenge of working it out from day to day in practical living. How are we to do this? The answer is simple: by faith. This truth, too, is contained in Paul's opening theme: *"The righteous man shall live by faith"* (Romans 1:17). Viewed from a practical standpoint, the verb *live* is one of the most all-inclusive words we can use. Everything we do at any time is included in living: eating, drinking, sleeping, working, and the innumerable other activities of life. Through faith, every one of these commonplace activities can become a way to express the life of God that we have received within us.

We are often prone to assume that the mundane actions of daily life have no spiritual significance and offer no place for the application of our faith. But Scripture actually teaches the opposite. It is only after we have successfully applied our faith in the

FAITH IS THE ONLY BASIS FOR
RIGHTEOUS LIVING.

simple, material areas of life that God will promote us to higher spiritual responsibilities. Jesus Himself laid down this principle:

> He who is faithful in a very little thing is faithful also in much; and he who is unrighteous in a very little thing is unrighteous also in much. If therefore you have not been faithful in the use of unrighteous mammon [money], who will entrust the true riches to you?　　　　　　　　　　　(Luke 16:10–11)

Only after we have made our faith work in the *"very little thing*[s]," and in the area of money, will God entrust to us the greater responsibilities and the true spiritual riches.

Therefore, in examining how we can work out our faith in daily living, we will consider two practical, down-to-earth areas: food and finance. From many years of personal observation, I have concluded that a believer who has learned to apply his faith in these two areas is likely to be leading a successful Christian life. On the other hand, if a person has not brought these basic areas under God's control, it is usually an indication that his whole life needs to be adjusted.

EATING FROM FAITH

I have stated already that the third movement of the symphony of the book of Romans, which begins at chapter twelve, focuses on the practical application of our faith. What does it start with? Something remote or ethereal? No! On the contrary, it begins, in the very first verse, with our bodies:

> I urge you therefore, brethren, by the mercies of God, to present your bodies a living and holy sacrifice, acceptable to God, which is your spiritual service of worship.　　(Romans 12:1)

Paul told us that our *"spiritual service of worship"* consists of presenting our bodies to God. In other words, to be "spiritual" is to be very practical and down-to-earth. It begins with what we do with our bodies.

From this starting point, Paul went on to deal with a variety of practical issues related to the Christian life. In chapter fourteen, he dealt with the issue of food. (Obviously, there is no issue of greater importance to our physical bodies than this!) He wrote about two types of believers: *"One man has faith that he may eat all things, but he who is weak eats vegetables only"* (Romans 14:2). Paul did not settle this issue by saying that it is absolutely right to eat vegetables and absolutely wrong to eat meat, or vice versa. Rather, he said that anything we can do in faith is right, and anything we cannot do in faith is wrong. He stated his conclusion in the closing verse of the chapter: *"But he who doubts is condemned if he eats, because his eating is not from faith; and whatever is not from faith is sin"* (verse 23).

By his closing statement, Paul went beyond the mere issue of eating meat or vegetables and reaffirmed the principle that had been the opening theme of his epistle. In Romans 1:17, he had stated it in positive terms: *"The righteous man shall live by faith."* Here, in Romans 14:23, he stated the same principle in negative terms: *"Whatever is not from faith is sin."* Viewed positively or negatively, the conclusion is the same: faith is the only basis for righteous living.

Let us then accept this challenge of applying our faith to our eating. We are required to "eat from faith." This is a rather strange phrase. How can we apply it in a practical way?

Several things are involved. First of all, we must acknowledge our dependence on God for our food. We receive it as a gift from Him. If He did not supply it, we would go hungry.

Second, as a logical consequence, we thank God for our food. Thanking God for our food, in turn, produces a third consequence, which Paul explained in 1 Timothy:

For everything created by God is good, and nothing is to be rejected, if it is received with gratitude [literally, thanksgiving]; for it is sanctified by means of the word of God and prayer.   (1 Timothy 4:4–5)

As we receive our food from God with prayers of thanksgiving, it is sanctified; it actually becomes holy, designed by God to do us good. Even if there are impure or harmful ingredients in our food, their effect is nullified by our faith, which is expressed in our prayers of thanksgiving.

Fourth, "eating from faith" has implications that go beyond the supper table. Our food is the source of our natural strength, and God is the source of our food. Therefore, our strength itself is a gift from God. We are not free to use it in selfish or sinful ways, but we are under an obligation to devote it to God's service and God's glory.

As we apply the principle of faith to our eating, this whole area of our lives gains a new significance. We can understand how Paul could instruct the believers at Corinth with the following exhortation: *"Whether, then, you eat or drink or whatever you do, do all to the glory of God"* (1 Corinthians 10:31). Through faith, even our daily meals take on the nature of a sacrament, of which we partake for God's glory. This was one of the most immediate and obvious effects produced in the lives of the first Christians by the outpouring of the Holy Spirit on the day of Pentecost. Their meals became spiritual feasts of worship and praise. Luke recorded the following:

And day by day continuing with one mind in the temple, and breaking bread from house to house, they were taking their meals together with gladness and sincerity of heart, praising God, and having favor with all the people. And the Lord was adding to their number day by day those who were being saved.   (Acts 2:46–47)

FAITH IS THE CHANNEL
OF DIVINE LIFE:
THE MORE FAITH WE EXERCISE,
THE MORE LIFE WE ENJOY.

The way these Christians ate their meals was so different that it gained them the favor of their unconverted neighbors—and won those neighbors to the Lord. It can be the same with us today, when we put our faith to work in this area of eating.

If the consequences of "eating from faith" are so far-reaching, what about the consequences of failing to eat in this way? For a vivid picture of the man who does *not* eat from faith, we may turn to the book of Ecclesiastes. Throughout most of the book, Solomon described what the Bible elsewhere calls the "natural man"—that is, the man who, through unbelief, lives his life without the grace and the knowledge of God. In Ecclesiastes 5:17, Solomon pictured such a man at the supper table: *"Throughout his life he also eats in darkness with great vexation, sickness and anger."*

What striking language! *"He…eats in darkness."* What does it mean? It means just the opposite of "eating from faith." Such a man does not acknowledge that his food is a gift from God. He does not thank God for it. Therefore, it is not blessed and sanctified. What is the result? *"Great vexation, sickness and anger."* To eat without faith is to invite vexation, sickness, and anger.

We have just examined rather carefully how the principle of faith applies to one of our most common daily activities—eating. As a result, we are in a position to understand more fully the scope of Romans 1:17: *"The righteous man shall live by faith."* Faith, we can now see, is the channel of divine life. The more faith we exercise, the more life we enjoy. Every activity to which we apply our faith becomes permeated with divine life. It is no longer drab or commonplace. It becomes fresh, exciting, joyous—an occasion for worship and praise!

FAITH FOR FINANCES

Another area of everyday living in which we need to apply the principle of faith is that of financial and material provision.

ABUNDANCE MEANS THAT GOD
SUPPLIES ALL WE NEED—WITH
SOMETHING TO SPARE FOR OTHERS.

The whole Bible abounds with both assurances and examples of God's ability to provide for His people's needs, even in situations in which there is no human or natural source of supply. Nowhere is this more emphatically stated than in 2 Corinthians 9:8: *"And God is able to make all grace abound to you, that always having all sufficiency in everything, you may have an abundance for every good deed."*

It is worthwhile to examine this verse closely. Where the English translation uses the words *"everything"* and *"every,"* the original Greek uses the word *all*. Thus, in the original text, the word *abound,* or *abundance,* occurs twice, and the word *all* occurs five times. It is hard to see how language could more forcefully express the ability of God to provide for every area of His people's needs. The level of provision He reveals is not mere sufficiency; it is *abundance*.

There are actually three levels of provision on which people may live: insufficiency, sufficiency, and abundance. Let me illustrate these three levels from the simple, everyday example of a homemaker shopping for groceries. A homemaker who needs fifteen dollars' worth of groceries and has ten dollars in her purse is shopping out of *insufficiency*. A homemaker who needs fifteen dollars' worth of groceries and has fifteen dollars in her purse is shopping out of *sufficiency*. But a homemaker who needs fifteen dollars' worth of groceries and has twenty dollars in her purse is shopping out of *abundance*.

In this rather simple example, we have pictured a homemaker buying groceries with dollars. However, it must be emphasized that abundance does not necessarily depend on money or material possessions. Abundance means simply that God supplies all we need—with something to spare for others. The perfect example of this form of abundance is provided by Jesus Himself. He had no permanent dwelling, no material possessions, and no large sums of money—although His disciple Judas did carry a money box in

THE BASIS OF OUR PROVISION
IS GOD'S GRACE,
NOT OUR WISDOM OR ABILITY.

which contributions were placed. (See John 12:4–6; 13:29.) Yet Jesus never lacked anything for Himself or for those who were with Him.

When Peter needed money on short notice to pay taxes, Jesus did not tell him to go and ask Judas for money out of the box. Instead, He sent him to the Sea of Galilee to collect it from a fish's mouth. (See Matthew 17:24–27.) This raises an interesting question. Which would be better: to go to the bank and cash a check or to go to the sea and cast in a hook? Certainly the latter would be much more exciting!

On another occasion, Jesus found Himself surrounded by a crowd of perhaps twelve thousand hungry people. We know that there were about five thousand men, and this figure does not include the women and children. (See Matthew 14:21.) Accepting five loaves and two fishes from a boy, Jesus gave thanks for them to His Father. As a result, He was able to feed the whole crowd, with twelve large basketfuls leftover. (See John 6:5–13.) That is abundance! It is also a startling demonstration of the supernatural effects of thanking God in faith for our food!

Later, Jesus sent His disciples out to begin preaching, but He told them not to take any extra supplies with them. (See Luke 9:1–3; 10:1–4.) At the end of His earthly ministry, He reminded them of this and asked them whether they had lacked anything. They replied, *"No, nothing"* (Luke 22:35). That is abundance! I myself have served as a missionary at various times in two different countries. I know from personal observation that it is possible for a missionary to be supplied with a house, a car, and a salary, and yet lack many things that he needs. The key to abundance is not money or material possessions. It is faith!

Confronted by these examples from the life of Jesus, we might at first be tempted to say, "But that was Jesus! We can't expect to be like Him!" However, Jesus Himself told us otherwise. In John 14:12, He said, *"Truly, truly, I say to you, he who believes in Me, the works that I do shall he do also.*" Likewise, the apostle John, who was an eyewitness of all that Jesus did, declared, "*The one who says he abides in Him ought himself to walk in the same manner as He walked*" (1 John 2:6). Jesus set the pattern for the walk of faith, and we are invited to follow.

If we still hesitate to accept this challenge, it may be because we do not comprehend the scope of God's grace. In 2 Corinthians 9:8, the key word is "*grace*": "*God is able to make all grace abound to you.*" The basis of our provision is not our own wisdom or ability, but God's grace. In order to avail ourselves of His grace, we need to understand two key principles that govern the operation of grace.

The first principle is stated in John 1:17: "*For the law was given through Moses; grace and truth came through Jesus Christ*" (NIV). Grace has only one channel—Jesus Christ. It is not received through the observance of any legal or religious system of rules, but solely and invariably through Christ.

The second principle is stated in Ephesians 2:8–9: "*For by grace you have been saved through faith;…not as a result of works, that no one should boast.*" Grace goes beyond anything that we can ever achieve or earn simply by our own abilities. Therefore, the only means by which we can appropriate it is faith. As long as we limit ourselves merely to what we deserve or what we can earn, we are failing to exercise faith, and therefore we do not enjoy God's grace to the full.

How do these principles apply in the area of our finances? First of all, I must emphasize that God never blesses dishonesty, laziness, or financial irresponsibility. In Proverbs 10:4, we are told, "*Lazy hands make a man poor, but diligent hands bring wealth*" (NIV). In the book of Ephesians, Paul said,

> *Let him who steals steal no longer; but rather let him labor, performing with his own hands what is good, in order that he may have something to share with him who has need.*
>
> (Ephesians 4:28)

God expects us, according to our abilities, to engage in honest work, not merely to earn enough for ourselves, but also to have something leftover to share with others who are in need. In 2 Thessalonians 3:10, Paul was even more emphatic: *"If anyone will not work, neither let him eat."* The provision of God's grace is not offered to the dishonest or the lazy.

However, it may be that, when we have honestly and conscientiously done everything in our power to provide for ourselves and our dependents, we still find ourselves on the level of bare sufficiency, or even of insufficiency. The message of grace is that we do not need to accept this state as being God's will. We can turn our faith to God through Jesus Christ and trust Him to lift us—by ways of His own choosing—onto a higher level of provision than we could ever achieve merely by our own wisdom or ability.

GOD'S PROVISION IS CORPORATE

Before we leave the subject of provision, there is one more very important principle that we need to recognize: God's provision for His people is corporate. He does not treat us simply as isolated individuals, but as members of a single body, bound to one another by strong ties of mutual commitment. In Ephesians, after presenting Christ as the Head of this body, Paul described how God intends the body to function:

> *From whom the whole body, being fitted and held together by that which every joint supplies, according to the proper working of each individual part, causes the growth of the body for the building up of itself in love.* (Ephesians 4:16)

Paul here emphasized the importance of the joints. They serve two functions: First, they hold the body together. Second, they are the channels of supply.

The joints represent the relationships among the various members. If these are in good shape, God's supply is able to reach every

GOD TREATS US AS MEMBERS OF
A BODY BOUND TOGETHER BY
STRONG TIES OF COMMITMENT.

part of the body, and no member suffers lack. But if the joints are not working properly—that is, if the members are not rightly related to one another—then there will be some parts of the body of Christ that will suffer lack. This will happen not because God's supply is inadequate, but only because our wrong attitudes and relationships hinder His supply from reaching some who need it.

In the Old Testament, when God delivered Israel out of Egypt, He taught them this principle in a very practical way. Two or three million people found themselves in a barren wilderness, without any normal food supply. To meet their needs, God caused manna to fall each night. In the morning, the people had to go out and gather it before the sun caused it to melt. The actual amount that each person needed was an omer, which is about two quarts. As it worked out, some Israelites gathered more than an omer, others less. Then they shared with each other and discovered that each one had just enough—precisely one omer! (See Exodus 16:14–18.) However, if they had not been willing to share in this way, some would not have had enough. Obviously, God could have arranged for each individual to gather as much as he needed for himself. But He did not do so because He wanted to teach His people their responsibility for one another.

This principle was carried on into the New Testament. In 2 Corinthians, Paul wrote about a special collection that he was receiving in the churches of Macedonia and Achaia on behalf of the poor Jewish believers in Judea. He explained to the Corinthians that this was God's way of providing equally for the various parts of the body of Christ without depriving some or overburdening others. To enforce this principle, he alluded to the example of the Israelites sharing their manna in the wilderness in this way:

> *There is no question of relieving others at the cost of hardship to yourselves; it is a question of equality. At the moment your surplus meets their need, but one day your need may be met from their surplus. The aim is equality; as Scripture has it,*

"The man who got much had no more than enough, and the man who got little did not go short."

(2 Corinthians 8:13–15 NEB)

In verse fifteen, Paul was referring to the Exodus passage:

Those who had gathered more had not too much, and those who had gathered less had not too little. (Exodus 16:18 NEB)

Christians are to share. It was by sharing that the congregation of the first Christians actually functioned in Jerusalem after the Holy Spirit was poured out upon them. Luke recorded the following:

And the congregation of those who believed were of one heart and soul; and not one of them claimed that anything belonging to him was his own; but all things were common property to them. And with great power the apostles were giving witness to the resurrection of the Lord Jesus, and abundant grace was upon them all. For there was not a needy person among them, for all who were owners of land or houses would sell them and bring the proceeds of the sales, and lay them at the apostles' feet; and they would be distributed to each, as any had need.

(Acts 4:32–35)

There are three statements here that go together. First, *"the apostles were giving witness to the resurrection of the Lord Jesus."* Second, *"abundant grace was upon them all."* Third, *"there was not a needy person among them."* The verbal witness of the apostles was strengthened by the visible grace of God upon the believers, and the practical result was that all their needs were met. In this way, the whole body of God's people provided a single, consistent testimony to the complete sufficiency of His grace in every area of their lives.

The world of our day needs a similar demonstration. People need to see a company of Christians who are so related to God through faith in Christ, and to one another by mutual commitment, that all their needs are met.

NO ALTERNATIVE TO FAITH

There are two sides to our relationship with God. Scripture is equally emphatic about each. On the positive side, as we have seen, God makes His abundant grace available to us on the basis of our faith. But on the negative side, God rejects any other basis on which we might seek to approach Him. Nowhere is this stated more forcefully than in the book of Hebrews:

> And without faith it is impossible to please Him, for he who comes to God must believe that He is, and that He is a rewarder of those who seek Him.   (Hebrews 11:6)

Left to ourselves, if we were asked what we need to do to please God, few of us would offer the answer that Scripture gives here. More often than not, people try to please God on some basis other than faith: by morality, by good works, by church membership, by charitable contributions, by prayer, or by other religious activities. But without faith, none of these is acceptable to God. No matter what else we do, no matter how good our motives, no matter how sincere or zealous we may be, there is no substitute for faith. Without it, we cannot please God. It is impossible!

Therefore, we find ourselves face-to-face with God's single, unvarying requirement: "He who comes to God must believe." There are two things that we are required to believe. First, we must believe that God exists. Most people believe that He exists, but that by itself is not sufficient. We must also believe that God is the "rewarder of those who seek Him." This goes beyond the fact of God's existence to His nature. We are required to believe in the essential goodness of God—His faithfulness and dependability.

THE ULTIMATE OBJECT
OF FAITH IS NONE OTHER THAN
GOD HIMSELF.

Believing in God in this way takes us beyond mere doctrine or theology. It establishes a direct, personal relationship between God and the one who believes.

In chapter one of this book, I said that faith connects us to two invisible realities: God and His Word. Now we must go one step further. The ultimate object of faith is none other than God Himself. It is true that we believe in God's Word, but we do so because His Word is an extension of Himself. Our confidence in His Word rests on our confidence in Him as a person. If we ever cease to believe in God, we will eventually cease to believe His Word, also.

It is very important to see that merely believing a form of doctrine or theology is not the ultimate goal. Those whose faith goes no further than this never come to know the fullness and richness of life that God offers us. His final purpose is to bring us into an immediate, intimate, person-to-person relationship with Himself. Once established, this relationship motivates, directs, and sustains all that we do. It becomes both the source and the consummation of life. Interpreted in this way, Habakkuk's prophecy *"The righteous will live by his faith"* (Habakkuk 2:4) points us not to a creed or a theology, but to an intimate, ongoing, all-embracing relationship with God Himself.

It is this kind of relationship that David spoke of in Psalm 23:1: *"The Lord is my shepherd, I shall not want."* David was not explaining a theology; he was describing a relationship. On the basis of his relationship to the Lord as his Shepherd, he declared, *"I shall not want."* What a marvelous expression of total personal security! It covers every need, every situation. David could have added other words; he could have said, "I will not lack money, food, friends, or health." But to do so would have weakened his words. *"I shall not want"* stands best alone, leaving no room for lack of any kind.

LIVING BY FAITH IS AN INTIMATE,
ONGOING, ALL-EMBRACING
RELATIONSHIP WITH GOD.

I am impressed by the way in which Scripture expresses the most profound truths in the simplest language. In the original Hebrew, Psalm 23:1 contains merely four words. In the *New American Standard Bible*, there are only nine words, and only one of them contains more than one syllable. Yet these few short words describe a relationship so deep and so strong that it takes care of every need that can ever arise—in life and in death, in time and in eternity.

THE BASIC SIN: UNBELIEF

We have seen that righteousness proceeds always and only from faith. We will now see that the opposite is also true; sin has only one ultimate source: unbelief.

In John 16:8, Jesus said that the ministry of the Holy Spirit would be to convict the world concerning three things: *"And He, when He comes, will convict the world concerning sin, and righteousness, and judgment."* Then, in the next verse, Jesus defined the specific sin of which the Holy Spirit would bring conviction: *"Concerning sin, because they do not believe in Me."* The primary sin, of which the whole world is guilty, is unbelief. This is the basis of all other sins.

The third chapter of Hebrews deals specifically with this sin of unbelief. The writer reminded us that a whole generation of God's people came out of Egypt under Moses, but they never entered the Promised Land because of their unbelief. Instead, they perished in the wilderness.

In Hebrews 3:12, the writer applied the tragic lesson that Israel learned to us as Christians: *"Take care, brethren, lest there should be in any one of you an evil, unbelieving heart, in falling away from the living God."* Most Christians tend to view unbelief as something regrettable, but comparatively harmless. However, we are told here that an unbelieving heart is an evil heart. Unbelief is evil because it causes us to fall away from God. Just as faith establishes a personal relationship with God, so unbelief destroys it. The two are exactly opposite in their effects.

The writer continued: *"But encourage one another day after day, as long as it is still called 'Today,' lest any one of you be hardened by the deceitfulness of sin"* (Hebrews 3:13). Unbelief causes our hearts to become hardened toward God and thus exposes us to the deception of sin and of Satan. This warning against the danger of unbelief is an urgent one. The writer applies it to *"Today."* It concerns us Christians today no less than the Israelites who came out of Egypt under Moses. The effects of unbelief are as deadly for us as they were for them.

Finally, the writer summed up Israel's failure and stated its cause:

> *And with whom was He* [God] *angry for forty years? Was it not with those who sinned, whose bodies fell in the wilderness? And to whom did He swear that they should not enter His rest, but to those who were disobedient? And so we see that they were not able to enter because of unbelief.*
>
> (Hebrews 3:17–19)

Note the closing words: *"because of unbelief."* These Israelites had been guilty of many sins, including fornication, idolatry, complaining, rebellion, and so on. But the specific sin that kept them from entering their inheritance was unbelief. Unbelief is the source of all other sins. This can be demonstrated logically, once we understand that true faith is based ultimately on the nature of God Himself.

If we had complete and unreserved faith in three aspects of God's nature—His goodness, His wisdom, and His power—then we would never disobey Him. If, in every situation, we could believe that God is good, that He wants only the best for us, that He has the wisdom to know what is best and the power to provide it, then we would never have any motive for disobedience. All disobedience against God, traced back to its origin, comes from unbelief.

Only two attitudes toward God are possible: faith that unites us to Him or unbelief that separates us from Him. Each excludes the other. The writer of the book of Hebrews quoted Habakkuk's prophecy, confronting us with the two alternatives:

> *But My righteous one shall live by faith; and if he shrinks back, My soul has no pleasure in him. But we are not of those who shrink back to destruction, but of those who have faith to the preserving of the soul.*   (Hebrews 10:38–39)

Once we have committed ourselves to the life that is based on faith, we cannot afford to turn away from it again. To go back into unbelief leads only to darkness and destruction. To go forward, we must continue as we began—in faith!

SUMMARY

The New Testament message of salvation and righteousness is based on Habakkuk 2:4: *"But the righteous will live by his faith."* Through faith in Jesus Christ, we receive from God, here and now, a new kind of life—divine, eternal, righteous. Thereafter, as we go on to apply our faith to the various areas of our lives, they are permeated and transformed by this new life from God.

The principle of faith must be made to work in simple, practical matters. In Romans 14, Paul applied it to eating. He discussed the case of two believers who disagreed about what may or may not be eaten. He concluded that what matters is not what we eat, but whether we "eat from faith."

"Eating from faith" has the following implications. First, we receive our food as a gift from God. Second, we thank God for it. Third, our food is thus sanctified. Fourth, we devote the strength we receive from it to God's service and God's glory. In

THE EFFECTS OF UNBELIEF ARE
AS DEADLY FOR US AS THEY WERE
FOR THE ISRAELITES.

this way, faith transforms the commonplace activity of eating into a sacrament.

Another practical area in which we need to apply our faith is that of financial and material provision. Through Christ, God's grace makes abundance available to us. That is, He promises that all our needs will be supplied and that we will have something leftover for others. However, abundance does not depend on money or material possessions, but solely on faith. The pattern of having abundance without money or possessions is provided by Jesus Himself, and we are challenged to follow His example. At the same time, we are strongly warned against laziness, dishonesty, and irresponsibility.

In order for all of God's people to partake of His abundance, we need to see ourselves not just as isolated individuals, but as members of a single body. God taught the Israelites this lesson by the manna with which He fed them in the wilderness. In order for each one to have enough, they all had to share what they had gathered. So it is with the body of Christ. If our attitudes and relationships are right, we share with each other, and there is enough for all. But wrong attitudes and relationships can shut off some areas of the body from receiving their full supply.

After the Holy Spirit was poured out upon the first Christians in Jerusalem, the practical outworking of their faith was manifested in both of the areas we have considered: food and finance. Their meals became sacraments, accompanied by praise and worship. They made their finances available to each other in such a way that "there was not a needy person among them" (Acts 4:34). God's grace thus manifested in their daily lives helped to win their neighbors to Christ.

God offers us nothing other than faith as the basis on which to approach Him. Nor is it enough to believe simply in His existence. We must believe in His essential goodness. This takes us beyond mere theology into a direct, intimate relationship with God as a person, which becomes our guarantee of total provision and total security.

Sin has only one ultimate source: unbelief. If we were to have complete, unvarying faith in God's goodness, wisdom, and power, we would never have any motive for sin. The writer of Hebrews pointed out that it was unbelief that kept the Israelites out of their inheritance, and he warned us as Christians about making the same deadly error. In the final analysis, there are only two possible attitudes toward God: faith that unites us to Him or unbelief that separates us from Him.

6

HOW FAITH COMES

In the previous chapter, we faced the challenge of God's uncompromising demands for faith: *"The righteous man shall live by faith"* (Romans 1:17). *"Whatever is not from faith is sin"* (Romans 14:23). *"Without faith it is impossible to please Him"* (Hebrews 11:6). *"He who comes to God must believe"* (verse 6). In light of these divine demands, we can easily see why Scripture compares faith to precious gold. Its value is unique. There is no substitute for it. Without faith, we cannot approach God, we cannot please Him—and we cannot receive His life.

How, then, do we acquire faith? Is it something unpredictable and unexplainable over which we have no control? Or does the same Bible that presents God's demands for faith also show us the way to obtain it?

It is my purpose in this chapter to share one of the most important discoveries I have ever made in the Christian life. Like most of the lessons that have proved of permanent value to me, I learned it the hard way—by personal experience. Out of a period of struggle and suffering, I eventually emerged with this one pearl of great price: I had learned how faith comes.

LIGHT IN A DARK VALLEY

During my service with the British army in World War II, I lay sick with a chronic skin infection for twelve months in a military

IF YOU DO NOT HAVE FAITH,
YOU CAN GET IT!

hospital in Egypt. Month by month, I became more convinced that the doctors did not have the means to cure me in the hot desert climate. Having recently become a Christian and having been baptized in the Holy Spirit, I had a real, personal relationship with God. I felt that somehow He must have the answer to my problem, but I did not know how to find it.

Over and over again, I said to myself, *I know that if I had faith, God would heal me.* Then I always added, *But I don't have faith.* Each time I said that, I found myself in what John Bunyan, in his book *The Pilgrim's Progress,* called the "Slough of Despond"—the dark, lonely valley of despair. One day, however, a brilliant ray of light pierced the darkness. I was in bed, propped up by my pillows, holding my Bible open across my knees, when my eyes were suddenly arrested by Romans 10:17: *"So then faith cometh by hearing, and hearing by the word of God"* (KJV). A single word gripped my attention. It was *"cometh."* I laid hold of one simple fact: *"Faith cometh"*! If I did not have faith, I could get it!

But how does faith come? I read the verse again: *"Faith cometh by hearing, and hearing by the word of God."* I had already accepted the Bible as the Word of God, so the source of faith was right there in my hands. But what was meant by *"hearing"*? How could I "hear" what the Bible had to say to me?

I determined to go back to the beginning of the Bible and read it right through, book by book, in order. At the same time, I armed myself with a blue pencil, intending to underline in blue every verse that dealt with the following themes: healing, health, physical strength, and long life. At times the going was not easy, but I persevered. I was surprised at how often I needed to use my blue pencil!

After about two months, I reached the book of Proverbs. There, in the fourth chapter, I found three consecutive verses that required my blue pencil:

> *My son, attend to my words; incline thine ear unto my sayings.*
> *Let them not depart from thine eyes; keep them in the midst*
> *of thine heart. For they are life unto those that find them, and*
> *health to all their flesh.*   (Proverbs 4:20–22 KJV)

As I was underlining these words, their meaning began to open up to me. "*My son.*" Through this passage, my Father, God, was speaking directly to me, His child. The message was very personal. God was telling me what His "*words*" and His "*sayings*" could be to me: "*health to all* [my] *flesh.*" How could God promise me more for my physical body than that? Health and sickness are opposites; each excludes the other. If I could have health in all my flesh—my whole physical body—then there would be no room for sickness in it anywhere.

I noticed that in the margin of my Bible, there was an alternative translation for "*health.*" It was "*medicine.*" Could God's "*words*" and "*sayings*" really be medicine for the healing of my whole body? After much inward debate, I determined to put this idea to the test. At my own request, all my medication was suspended. Then I began to take God's Word as my medicine. Since I was a hospital attendant by my military trade, I was familiar with the way people usually take their medicine: "three times daily after meals." I decided to take God's Word as my medicine that way.

When I made that decision, God spoke to my mind with words as clear as if I had heard them audibly: "When the doctor gives a person medicine, the directions for taking it are on the bottle. This passage in Proverbs is My medicine bottle, and the directions are on it. You had better read them."

Reading Proverbs 4:20–22 (KJV) carefully through once more, I saw that there are four directions for taking God's medicine:

1. "*Attend*" (verse 20). I must give undivided, concentrated attention to God's words as I read them.

2. *"Incline thine ear"* (verse 20). Inclining my ear would indicate a humble, teachable attitude. I must lay aside my own prejudices and preconceptions and receive with an open mind what God is saying to me.

3. *"Let them not depart from thine eyes"* (verse 21). I must keep my eyes focused on God's words. I must not allow my eyes to wander to other statements from conflicting sources, such as books or articles not based on Scripture.

4. *"Keep them in the midst of thine heart"* (verse 21). Even when the actual words are no longer in front of my eyes, I must keep meditating on them in my heart, thus keeping them at the very source and center of my life.

To describe all that happened in the following months would almost require a book of its own. The army transferred me from Egypt to the Sudan, a land with one of the worst climates in Africa, where temperatures reach as high as 127 degrees. Excessive heat had always aggravated my skin condition. Everything in my circumstances was opposed to my healing. Healthy men all around me were becoming sick. Gradually, however, I realized that the fulfillment of God's promises does not depend on external circumstances, but solely on meeting His conditions. So I simply continued to take my "medicine" three times daily. After each main meal, I would bow my head over my open Bible and say, "Lord, You have promised that these words of Yours will be medicine to all my flesh. I'm taking them as my medicine now—in the name of Jesus!"

No sudden or dramatic change took place. I experienced nothing that I could describe as a miracle. But after I had been in the Sudan for about three months, I discovered that my medicine had made good its claims. I was perfectly well. There was no more sickness anywhere in my body. I had actually received *"health to all* [my] *flesh"* (Proverbs 4:22 KJV).

GOD'S PROMISES DO NOT DEPEND
ON EXTERNAL CIRCUMSTANCES,
BUT ON MEETING HIS CONDITIONS.

This was not a case of "mind over matter"—some kind of temporary illusion that would quickly fade. Over fifty years have passed since then, and, with few exceptions, I have continued to enjoy excellent health. Looking back, I realize that through my period of testing and eventual victory, I made contact with a source of life above the natural level that is still at work in my physical body today.

LOGOS AND *RHEMA*

I have described the steps that led me to healing and health because they illustrate certain deep, enduring principles concerning the nature of God's Word. In the original Greek of the New Testament, there are two different words that are normally translated "word." One is *logos*; the other is *rhema*. At times these two words are used interchangeably. Yet each has a distinct, special significance of its own.

The word *logos* means more than a word that is spoken or written. It denotes those functions that are the expression of a mind. The authoritative Greek lexicon of Liddell and Scott defines *logos* as "the power of the mind that is manifested in speech; reason." In this sense, *logos* is the unchanging Word of God. It is God's counsel, settled in eternity before time began, and due to continue on into eternity long after time has run its course. It was of this divine *logos* that the psalmist was speaking when he said, *"Forever, O LORD, Thy word is settled in heaven"* (Psalm 119:89). Nothing that happens on earth can ever affect or change this word that is eternal in heaven. On the other hand, the word *rhema* is derived from a verb meaning "to speak," and denotes specifically "a word that is spoken"—a word that occurs in time and space.

In Romans 10:17, when Paul said that *"faith cometh by hearing, and hearing by the word of God"* (KJV), he used the word *rhema*, not *logos*. This usage agrees with the fact that he coupled *"word"* with *"hearing."* Logically, in order to be heard, a word must be spoken.

GOD DIRECTS US TO CERTAIN
SCRIPTURES AND IMPARTS *RHEMA*
LIFE TO THEM SO WE CAN HEAR
AND RECEIVE THEM BY FAITH.

When I sat on my hospital bed in Egypt with my Bible open across my knees, all I had in front of me—from the material point of view—were white sheets of paper with black marks printed on them. But when I came to those verses in Proverbs 4 about God's words and sayings being health to all my flesh, they were no longer just black marks on white paper. The Holy Spirit took the very words that would meet my need at that moment and imparted His life to them. They became a *rhema*—something I could "hear"—a living voice speaking to my heart. God Himself was speaking directly and personally to me. As I heard His words, faith came to me through them.

This experience corresponds with Paul's statement in 2 Corinthians 3:6: "*The letter kills, but the Spirit gives life.*" Apart from the Holy Spirit, there can be no *rhema*. In the Bible, the *logos*—the total counsel of God—is made available to me. But *logos* is too vast and too complex for me to comprehend or assimilate in its totality. *Rhema* is the way that the Holy Spirit brings a portion of *logos* down out of eternity and relates it to time and human experience. *Rhema* is that portion of the total *logos* that applies at a certain point in time to my particular situation. Through *rhema*, *logos* is applied to my life and thus becomes specific and personal in my experience.

In the transaction between God and man through which faith comes, the initiative is with God. This leaves no room for arrogance or presumption on our part. Indeed, in Romans 3:27, Paul told us that boasting is excluded by the law of faith. It is God who knows—knows better than we do—just what part of the total *logos* will meet our need at any given time. By His Holy Spirit, He directs us to the very words that are appropriate and then imparts life to them so that they become a *rhema*—a living voice. At this point, the response required of us is hearing. To the extent that we hear, we receive faith.

EACH *RHEMA* WE RECEIVE IS
THE DAILY BREAD BY WHICH WE
SUSTAIN OUR SPIRITUAL LIVES.

———————

What is involved in hearing? It is important that we know as precisely as possible what is required of us. This, too, was included in the lesson I received there in my hospital bed. In the wisdom of God, the words that came to me from Proverbs 4 not only met my physical need, but they also provided a complete and detailed example of what it means to "hear" God's Word. As God pointed out to me, the directions on His medicine bottle are four-fold: first, *"attend"* (Proverbs 4:20 KJV); second, *"incline thine ear"* (verse 20 KJV); third, *"let them not depart from thine eyes"* (verse 21 KJV); fourth, *"keep them in the midst of thine heart"* (verse 21 KJV). Without realizing it at first, as I followed these four directions, I was hearing. As a result, faith came.

Hearing, then, consists of these four elements:

1. We give close, undivided attention to what God is saying to us by His Holy Spirit. By a firm decision of our wills, we exclude all extraneous, distracting influences.

2. We incline our ears. We adopt a humble, teachable attitude toward God. We renounce our own prejudices and preconceptions, and we accept what God says in its plainest and most practical meaning.

3. We focus our eyes on the word to which God has directed us. We do not allow our eyes to wander to statements from other sources that may conflict with what God is saying.

4. Even when the words are no longer before our eyes, we continue to meditate on them in our hearts. In this way, we retain them continually at the center of our beings, and their influence permeates every area of our lives.

As God's *rhema* comes to us in this way, it is both specific and personal. Let me illustrate this truth from my experience in the hospital. God spoke to me at that time as an individual in a specific situation. He showed me how to receive my healing: I was to

RHEMA BRINGS GOD'S WAYS AND
THOUGHTS TO US, REPLACING
OURS WITH HIS.

take His words as my medicine and forgo all normal medication. I obeyed, and I was healed. However, it would be wrong for me to assume that God would prescribe the same remedy for someone else—or even for me at another stage of my experience. In fact, on subsequent occasions when I have needed healing, God has not always directed me in the same way. There have been times when I have gratefully accepted the help of doctors and received healing that way.

Rhema, then, comes to each of us directly and individually from God. It is appropriate to a specific time and place. It presupposes an ongoing, personal relationship with God. By each successive *rhema,* God guides us in the individual walk of faith to which He has called us. A *rhema* that is given to one believer may not be appropriate for another. And, again, it may not even be appropriate for the same believer in another stage of his experience.

This life of continuing dependence on God's *rhema* is clearly set forth in the words with which Jesus answered Satan's first temptation in the wilderness: *"Man shall not live on bread alone, but on every word [rhema] that proceeds out of the mouth of God"* (Matthew 4:4). The word *"proceeds"* is in the continuous present tense. We could say, "Every word as it proceeds out of the mouth of God." Jesus here spoke of a specific word proceeding directly from God's mouth, a word energized by the breath of His mouth, or, in other words, by the Holy Spirit. This is our daily bread—always fresh, always "proceeding." As we live in continual dependence on God's *rhema,* day by day, it imparts to us the faith by which the righteous man lives.

We may sum up the relationship between *logos* and *rhema* in the following statements:

- *Rhema* takes the eternal *logos* and injects it into time.
- *Rhema* takes the heavenly *logos* and brings it down to earth.
- *Rhema* takes the potential *logos* and makes it actual.

"DO AS THOU HAST SPOKEN" IS
THE MOST EFFECTIVE PRAYER
ANYONE CAN PRAY.

+ *Rhema* takes the general *logos* and makes it specific.

+ *Rhema* takes a portion of the total *logos* and presents it in a form that an individual can comprehend and assimilate.

+ *Rhema* is like each of the broken pieces of bread with which Jesus fed the multitude—it is suited to each individual's need and capacity. Often it comes to us through another's hands.

FROM HEAVEN TO EARTH

The prophet Isaiah presented the relationship between *logos* and *rhema* in vivid imagery:

> *"For My thoughts are not your thoughts, neither are your ways My ways," declares the LORD. "For as the heavens are higher than the earth, so are My ways higher than your ways, and My thoughts than your thoughts. For as the rain and the snow come down from heaven, and do not return there without watering the earth, and making it bear and sprout, and furnishing seed to the sower and bread to the eater; so shall My word be which goes forth from My mouth; it shall not return to Me empty, without accomplishing what I desire, and without succeeding in the matter for which I sent it. For you will go out with joy, and be led forth with peace; the mountains and the hills will break forth into shouts of joy before you, and all the trees of the field will clap their hands. Instead of the thorn bush the cypress will come up; and instead of the nettle the myrtle will come up; and it will be a memorial to the LORD, for an everlasting sign which will not be cut off."* (Isaiah 55:8–13)

Here we have two different planes: the heavenly plane and the earthly plane. On the heavenly plane is the divine *logos*: God's ways and thoughts, the total counsel of God settled forever in heaven. On the earthly level are man's ways and thoughts, far below those of God and actually incompatible with them. There is no way by

EVERY *RHEMA* FROM GOD
CONTAINS THE POWER FOR ITS
OWN FULFILLMENT.

which man can rise from his level to God's level, but there is a way by which God's ways and thoughts can be brought down to man. God says that His word that goes forth from His mouth will be like the rain and the snow that bring heaven's life-giving moisture down to earth.

This is the same word that Jesus spoke of in Matthew 4:4, the "*word that proceeds out of the mouth of God*," the word by which man lives. It is a portion of the heavenly *logos* coming down to earth as *rhema*. It imparts to us the portion of God's ways and thoughts that applies to our situation and meets our need at that moment.

Received and obeyed, *rhema* brings forth in our lives the activity and the fruit that glorify God. We "*go out with joy*" (Isaiah 55:12); we are "*led forth with peace*" (verse 12). "*Instead of the thorn bush the cypress* [comes] *up; and instead of the nettle the myrtle* [comes] *up*" (verse 13). The "*thorn bush*" and the "*nettle*" typify our ways and our thoughts. As we receive the *rhema* from God's mouth, these are replaced by the "*cypress*" and the "*myrtle*," which typify God's ways and God's thoughts.

DAVID AND MARY, OUR EXAMPLES

To further illustrate the way that *rhema* comes and the results it produces, we will take two incidents from Scripture—one from the Old Testament, concerning David, and one from the New Testament, concerning the Virgin Mary.

In 1 Chronicles 17, we see David established as king over Israel—victorious, prosperous, and at ease. Contrasting his own luxurious palace with the humble tabernacle that still housed the sacred ark of God's covenant, he desired to build a temple worthy of God and His covenant. The prophet Nathan, with whom David shared his desire, at first gave him warm encouragement. But that night, God spoke to Nathan and sent him back to David with a different message. The message began, "*You shall not build a house for Me"* (verse 4), but it closed, *"Moreover, I tell you that the* LORD *will build a house for you"* (verse 10).

Here is an example of the difference between the ways and thoughts of God and of man. The highest plan that David could conceive was still on the earthly plane: that he would build a house for God. The promise that came back to him from God was on the heavenly plane, far higher than David would ever have conceived: that God would build a house for him. Furthermore, David had used the word *house* in its material sense, merely as a dwelling place. But in His promise, God used the word *house* in its wider meaning, the meaning of an enduring posterity—a royal line that would continue forever.

In his message, Nathan brought to David a *rhema*—a direct, personal word from God. In response, David *"went in and sat before the* LORD*"* (1 Chronicles 17:16). What was he doing? First of all, he had to set aside his own plans and preconceptions. Gradually, as he was emptied of these, he began to meditate with focused attention on God's message, allowing it to penetrate to his innermost being. In this condition of inner stillness, he was able to hear. Finally, out of hearing, faith came—the faith needed to appropriate what God had promised him. Still sitting in God's presence, David replied, *"And now, O* LORD, *let the word that Thou hast spoken concerning Thy servant and concerning his house, be established forever, and do as Thou hast spoken"* (verse 23).

"The word that Thou hast spoken"—that was the *rhema*. It did not originate on the earthly plane of David's own ways and thoughts. It came down from the heavenly plane, bringing God's ways and thoughts to David. Having heard this *rhema* and having allowed it to produce faith within him, David appropriated its promise by a prayer that included five short words: *"Do as Thou hast spoken."* These five words represent the most effective prayer that anyone can pray—so simple, so logical, and yet so powerful. Once we are truly convinced that God has said something to us,

and we in turn ask Him to do what He has said, how can we doubt that He will do it? What power in heaven or on earth can prevent it?

From David, we move on through a thousand years of Jewish history to a humble descendant of his royal line—a peasant maiden named Mary, who lived in the city of Nazareth. An angel appeared to her with a message from the throne of God:

> *And behold, you will conceive in your womb, and bear a son, and you shall name Him Jesus. He will be great, and will be called the Son of the Most High; and the Lord God will give Him the throne of His father David; and He will reign over the house of Jacob forever; and His kingdom will have no end.* (Luke 1:31–33)

When Mary questioned how this could come about, the angel explained that it would be by the supernatural power of the Holy Spirit. He concluded his message with the words, *"For nothing will be impossible with God"* (verse 37). In the original Greek, the word translated *"nothing"* literally means "no word"—"no *rhema*." The angel's reply could just as well be rendered, "No word (*rhema*) from God will be void of power" or, more freely, "Every word (*rhema*) from God contains the power for its own fulfillment."

The angel brought to Mary a *rhema*—a direct, personal word from God to her. That *rhema* contained in it the power to fulfill what it promised. The outcome depended on Mary's response. *"Behold, the bondslave of the Lord,"* she replied; *"be it done to me according to your word"* (verse 38). By these words, Mary unlocked the supernatural power of God in the *rhema* and opened herself to its fulfillment in her physical body. As a result, there occurred the greatest miracle of human history: the birth of God's eternal Son from the womb of a virgin.

In its simplicity, Mary's response was parallel to that of David. David said, *"Do as Thou hast spoken"* (1 Chronicles 17:23). Mary

RHEMA IS GOD'S WORD
PROCEEDING OUT OF
GOD'S MOUTH.

said, *"Be it done to me according to your word."* Both of these simple replies unlocked the miracle-working power of God to fulfill the promise that had been given. In both cases, the *rhema*, received by faith, contained in it the power for its own fulfillment.

Some people may question my statement that the miracle of Jesus's birth depended on the response of Mary's faith. Yet this truth is plainly indicated by the closing words of the salutation with which Elizabeth later greeted Mary: *"And blessed is she who believed that there would be a fulfillment of what had been spoken to her by the Lord"* (Luke 1:45). The implication is clear: The fulfillment of the promise came because Mary had believed it. Without this belief, there would have been no way for God's miracle-working power to fulfill what had been promised.

Let us see how the experiences of David and of Mary parallel each other:

1. To both of them, there came a *rhema*—a direct, personal word from God.

2. This *rhema* expressed the ways and thoughts of God, which were far above anything that they would ever have conceived by their own reasoning or imagination.

3. As they heard the *rhema*, it imparted faith to them.

4. Both expressed faith by a simple statement that gave consent to what was promised: *"Do as Thou hast spoken"* (1 Chronicles 17:23). *"Be it done to me according to your word"* (Luke 1:38).

5. Faith expressed in this way made room for the power of God within the *rhema* to bring about the fulfillment of what had been promised.

God still works the same way today with His believing people. By the Holy Spirit, He takes out of His *logos*, His eternal counsel, a *rhema*—a specific word that fits a particular situation in time and

RHEMA IS GOD'S WORD
PROCEEDING OUT OF
GOD'S MOUTH.

space. As we "hear" this *rhema,* faith comes. Then, as we use the faith we have thus received to appropriate the *rhema,* we discover that the word from God contains in itself the power needed to work out its own fulfillment.

SUMMARY

The Bible presents God's demand for faith, but it also shows us how to acquire faith. Romans 10:17 (KJV) tells us that "*faith cometh by hearing*" God's word—God's *rhema*—His Word made alive and personal by the Holy Spirit.

We need to see the relationship between *logos* and *rhema. Logos* is God's unchanging counsel, settled forever in heaven. *Rhema* is the way the Holy Spirit brings a portion of *logos* down out of eternity and relates it to time and human experience. Through *rhema, logos* becomes specific and personal. As we hear this *rhema,* faith comes to us through it.

What is meant by "*hearing*"? A good, practical example is provided by Proverbs 4:20–22, which I refer to as "God's medicine bottle." The directions on the medicine bottle contain the four elements that constitute hearing: first, give close, undivided attention to what God is saying to you by the Holy Spirit; second, adopt a humble, teachable attitude; third, focus your eyes on the words to which God has directed you; and, fourth, continually meditate on them in your heart.

Rhema is God's word proceeding out of God's mouth. As we continue to hear each such word that comes to us, it provides the daily bread by which we maintain our spiritual life and our ongoing walk with God.

Rhema is also compared to the rain and snow that bring heaven's life-giving moisture down to earth, replacing barrenness with fruitfulness. *Rhema* brings God's ways and thoughts down to our human level and replaces our ways and thoughts with His.

Two examples of how *rhema* works are provided by King David and the Virgin Mary. David had planned to build a house for the Lord, but the Lord sent a *rhema*, saying that He would build a house for David. To Mary, God sent a *rhema* by the angel Gabriel, saying that she was to become the mother of Israel's long-awaited Messiah, the Son of God. In each case, as David and Mary heard the *rhema*, it imparted faith to them. Through faith, they were able to receive the fulfillment of what the *rhema* had promised. Their responses were simple but sufficient: *"Do as Thou hast spoken"* (1 Chronicles 17:23), and *"Be it done to me according to your word"* (Luke 1:38).

7

FAITH MUST BE CONFESSED

Once faith has come, there are three phases of development through which it must pass: confession, outworking, and testing. We may call these the three great "musts" of faith. Faith must be confessed with the mouth; faith must be worked out in action; faith must be tested by tribulation.

CONFESSION WITH THE MOUTH

The words *confess* and *confession* are important scriptural terms with a special meaning. The Greek verb *homologeo*, normally translated "to confess," means literally "to say the same as." Thus, confession is "saying the same as." However, translators sometimes use the related words *profess* and *profession* in place of *confess* and *confession*. The phrase "profess our faith" is widely used among many Christians and is synonymous with "confess our faith," which is the term I will use in this chapter. Regardless of which word is used, the basic meaning of *confess* and *profess* remains the same: "to say the same as."

In this special sense, confession is always related directly to God's Word. Confession is saying the same with our mouths as God says in His Word. It is making the words of our mouths agree with the written Word of God.

THE MOUTH IS THE OVERFLOW
VALVE OF THE HEART.

In Psalm 116:10, the psalmist said, *"I believed, therefore have I spoken"* (KJV). In 2 Corinthians 4:13, Paul applied these words to the confession of our faith: *"But having the same spirit of faith, according to what is written, 'I believed, therefore I spoke,' we also believe, therefore also we speak."* Speaking is the natural way for faith to express itself. Faith that does not speak is stillborn.

The whole Bible emphasizes that there is a direct connection between our mouths and our hearts. What happens in the one can never be separated from what happens in the other. In Matthew 12:34, Jesus told us, *"For the mouth speaks out of that which fills the heart."* *Today's English Version* renders this, *"For the mouth speaks what the heart is full of."* In other words, the mouth is the overflow valve of the heart. Whatever comes out through that overflow valve indicates the contents of the heart.

In the natural world, if the water that comes from the overflow valve of a cistern contains particles of grit or fungus, then it does no good to claim that the water in the cistern is pure. There must be grit or fungus somewhere in it. The same concept applies to the contents of our hearts. If our hearts are filled with faith, then that will be expressed in what we say with our mouths. But if words of doubt or unbelief come out of our mouths, they inevitably indicate that there is doubt or unbelief somewhere in our hearts.

As a hospital attendant with the British forces in North Africa, I worked closely with a Scottish doctor who was in charge of a small field hospital that cared only for dysentery cases. Every morning, as we made our rounds, the doctor invariably addressed each patient with the same two opening sentences: "How are you? Show me your tongue!"

As I participated in this medical ritual each day, I observed that the doctor was much more interested in the state of the patient's tongue than in the answer that he received to the question, "How are you?" I have reflected many times since then that the same is probably true of our relationship with God. We may offer God

WHENEVER FAITH AND FEELINGS
CONFLICT, WE MUST TAKE OUR
STAND WITH FAITH.

our own assessments of our spiritual conditions, but in the final analysis, God, like the doctor, judges mainly from our tongues.

As Paul defined the basic requirements for salvation, he laid equal stress on faith in the heart and confession with the mouth:

> *But what saith it? The word is nigh thee, even in thy mouth, and in thy heart: that is, the word of faith, which we preach; that if thou shalt confess with thy mouth the Lord Jesus, and shalt believe in thine heart that God hath raised him from the dead, thou shalt be saved. For with the heart man believeth unto righteousness; and with the mouth confession is made unto salvation.* (Romans 10:8–10 KJV)

I use the King James Version of these three verses because it is closer in structure and phraseology to the original Greek than any of the modern versions that I have discovered. In each of these three verses, Paul spoke about the mouth and the heart, but the order in which he did so is significant. In verse eight, it is the mouth first, then the heart. In verse nine, again it is the mouth first, then the heart. But in verse ten, the order is reversed: the heart comes first, then the mouth.

I believe that this ordering corresponds to our practical experience. We begin with God's Word in our mouths. By confessing it with our mouths, we receive it into our hearts. The more persistently we confess it with our mouths, the more firmly it becomes established in our hearts. Once faith is thus established in our hearts, no conscious effort is needed any longer to make the right confession. Faith naturally flows out in what we say with our mouths. Thereafter, as we continue to express our faith with our mouths, we confess our way progressively into the full benefits of salvation.

The way this process works was confirmed to me one day when I discovered that the phrase for "to learn by heart" in the Hebrew language is "to learn by mouth." I saw that the English phrase "to

WHEN WE SUBMIT TO GOD'S WILL,
WE HAVE SCRIPTURAL BASIS FOR
THE BENEFITS OF SALVATION.

learn by heart" describes the result that is to be achieved. The Hebrew phrase "to learn by mouth" describes the practical way in which we achieve that result. To learn things by heart, we repeat them with our mouths. We continue saying them over and over until doing so no longer requires any effort. In this way, what begins in our mouths eventually becomes permanently imprinted on our hearts.

This method was how, as a boy, I learned my multiplication tables. I kept repeating them over and over: seven times seven is forty-nine; seven times eight is fifty-six; seven times nine is sixty-three; and so on. Eventually I did not have to put forth any effort; I automatically thought of and spoke the answer. The truths of the multiplication tables were indelibly imprinted on my heart. They had become a part of me. Today, more than seventy years later, you may wake me in the middle of the night while a thunderstorm is raging and ask me, "What is seven times seven?" Although I may wonder why you are asking me this, I will reply without effort or hesitation, "Forty-nine."

In the same way, we can have the Word of God indelibly imprinted on our hearts. Each time a need arises, or our faith is challenged, we can confess God's Word as it applies to that situation. At first, there may be a struggle. Our feelings may prompt us to say something that does not agree with God's Word. But we must persistently resist our feelings and make the words of our mouths agree with God's Word. Eventually there will be no more struggle. It will be natural for us to say with our mouths, concerning each situation, the same thing that God says in His Word.

It is essential to distinguish between faith and feelings. Feelings are based on our senses. Many times their conclusions are contrary to God's Word. But faith, as we have already seen, connects us to the invisible realm of God and His Word. Whenever faith and feelings come into conflict, we must determine to take our stand—by confession—with faith, not feelings.

There are three words, each beginning with the letter *f,* that we must put in their right order: *facts, faith, feelings.* The *facts* are found in the Word of God, and they never vary. *Faith* takes its stand with the facts of God's Word and confesses them as true. *Feelings* may waver, but ultimately, if faith stands fast, feelings will come into alignment with the facts. On the other hand, if we start at the wrong end—with feelings rather than facts—we will always end up in trouble. Our feelings change hour by hour and moment by moment. If we base our lives on our feelings, our lives will be as unstable as our feelings are. *"The righteous man shall live by faith"* (Romans 1:17)—not feelings!

FIVE PRACTICAL SAFEGUARDS

This practice of persistently making the right confession with our mouths is very effective and very powerful. However, if perverted, it can lead to abuses that are spiritually dangerous. For instance, it may degenerate into a "mind over matter" type of approach. Such an approach was taught by the French philosopher Coue, whose remedy for life's problems was to keep repeating, "Every day, and in every way, I'm getting better and better." Another danger is that a zealous but immature Christian may imagine that he has found a way to twist God's arm, a way to compel the Almighty to meet his demands. Or our concept of God may be reduced to a kind of heavenly vending machine that needs only the right coin in the right slot to deliver the particular brand of carnal satisfaction that we select.

To avoid abuses of this kind, I suggest five scriptural safeguards. The first safeguard is this: We need to examine the attitudes with which we approach God. The writer of Hebrews made the following comment about the prayer that Jesus offered in the garden of Gethsemane: *"He was heard because of His reverent submission"* (Hebrews 5:7 NIV). Jesus's attitude of *"reverent submission"* was expressed in the words, *"Yet not My will, but Thine be done"* (Luke

22:42). These words set a pattern that we all must follow. Until we renounce our own wills and submit to God's will, we have no scriptural basis on which to claim the answers to our prayers or the benefits of our salvation.

The second safeguard is this: We are not free to confess just anything that we ourselves arbitrarily imagine or desire. Our confession must be kept within the limits of God's written Word. Any kind of confession that is not based directly on Scripture can easily develop into wishful thinking or fanaticism.

Here is the third safeguard: We can never cease to be dependent on the leading of the Holy Spirit. In Romans 8:14, Paul told us who the true sons of God are: *"For all who are being led by the Spirit of God, these are sons of God."* This leading applies as much to the confession that we make with our mouths as to any other aspect of the Christian life. The Holy Spirit must lead us to the particular area of scriptural truth that we need to confess in any given situation. In the previous chapter, we saw that only the Holy Spirit can take the eternal *logos* and apply it to each situation as a living, practical *rhema*.

The fourth safeguard is as follows: We never cease to be dependent on God's supernatural grace. In Ephesians 2:8, Paul stated a sequence that never varies: *"By grace...through faith."* It is always grace first, then faith. If we ever cease to depend on God's grace and power and begin to rely on our own abilities, the result in our experience will be the same as it was in Abraham's—an Ishmael, not an Isaac.

The fifth and final safeguard is this: It is important to correctly evaluate the evidence of our own senses. God does not ask us to close our eyes and ears and walk around as though the physical, material world around us does not exist. Faith is not mysticism. We do not question the *reality* of what our senses reveal, but we do question its *finality*.

WE DO NOT QUESTION
THE *REALITY* OF WHAT OUR
SENSES REVEAL, BUT WE
DO QUESTION ITS *FINALITY.*

In Romans chapter 4, Paul began by emphasizing that valid faith must always depend on God's grace. Then he showed us how Abraham resolved the tension between faith and the senses:

> *Therefore, the promise comes by faith, so that it may be by grace and may be guaranteed to all Abraham's offspring—not only to those who are of the law but also to those who are of the faith of Abraham. He is the father of us all. As it is written: "I have made you a father of many nations." He is our father in the sight of God, in whom he believed—the God who gives life to the dead and calls things that are not as though they were. Against all hope, Abraham in hope believed and so became the father of many nations, just as it had been said to him, "So shall your offspring be." Without weakening in his faith, he faced the fact that his body was as good as dead—since he was about a hundred years old—and that Sarah's womb was also dead. Yet he did not waver through unbelief regarding the promise of God, but was strengthened in his faith and gave glory to God, being fully persuaded that God had power to do what He had promised.* (Romans 4:16–21 NIV)

Abraham's senses told him that he was physically incapable of fathering a child and that Sarah was likewise incapable of bearing one. Yet God had promised them a son of their own. Abraham did not pretend that what his senses revealed to him about his own body and about Sarah's body was not real. He simply refused to accept it as final. When God's word promised him one thing and his senses told him another, he clung tenaciously to God's promise without letting his senses cause him to doubt that promise. Finally, after Abraham and Sarah's faith had been tested, their bodies were brought into alignment with what God had promised. They actually became physically capable of having a child.

It will be the same way with us. There may be a period of conflict between the statements of God's Word and what our senses tell us about a particular situation. But if our faith is valid, and if we cling to it as Abraham did, steadfastly maintaining the right confession, in due course the physical condition confronting us through our senses will be brought into line with what God's Word has to say about it.

CONFESSING UNTO SALVATION

We have seen that Paul concluded his teaching in Romans 10:8–10 with the statement, *"With the mouth confession is made unto salvation"* (verse 10 KJV). The word *"unto"* indicates motion, or progress. In other words, we move progressively forward into salvation as we continue making the right confession.

However, in order to make and maintain the right confession, we need to understand the scope of the word *salvation*. Many Christians limit confession to confessing their sins, and they limit salvation to having their sins forgiven. It is true that God does require us to confess our sins and that salvation includes having our sins forgiven. But the scope of both confession and salvation goes far beyond this.

In Psalm 78:22, we are told that God became angry with the Israelites after their deliverance from Egypt *"because they did not believe in God, and did not trust in His salvation."* The verses that precede and follow make it clear that God's *"salvation"* included all that He had done for Israel up to that point: His judgments on the Egyptians, the parting of the Red Sea, the cloud to guide them by day and the fire by night, the water that came from the rock for them to drink, and the manna that came from heaven for them to eat. These, and all God's other acts of intervention and provision on their behalf, are summed up in the single, all-inclusive word *salvation*.

In the New Testament, the Greek verb *sozo*—usually translated "to save"—goes far beyond the forgiveness of sins. It includes the meeting of every human need. Let me give just a few examples of its wider meaning. The word *sozo* is used for the healing of the woman suffering from a hemorrhage (see, for example, Matthew 9:20–22); the healing of the cripple at Lystra, lame from his mother's womb (see Acts 14:8–10); the deliverance of the Gerasene demoniac from a legion of demons and his restoration to his right mind (see, for example, Luke 8:26–36); the raising of the daughter of Jairus from the dead (see, for example, Luke 8:41–42, 49–55); and the restoration that comes from the prayer offered in faith on behalf of one who is sick (see James 5:14–15).

In addition, in 2 Timothy 4:18, Paul said, "*The Lord will deliver me from every evil deed, and will bring me safely to His heavenly kingdom.*" The word here translated "to bring safely" is *sozo*. In this context, *sozo* included every deliverance, protection, and provision of God needed to take Paul safely through his earthly life and to bring him at last into God's eternal kingdom.

Salvation includes all of the benefits purchased for us by the death of Christ on the cross. Whether these benefits are spiritual, physical, financial, material, temporal, or eternal, they are all summed up in one great, all-inclusive word—*salvation.*

The way we enter into and appropriate the various benefits of salvation is by confession. Scripture gives us clear, positive statements by which to lay hold of every area of God's provision. As we receive these by faith into our hearts and confess them with our mouths, we make them ours in actual experience.

For instance, Satan often assails Christians with feelings of condemnation and unworthiness. We may even begin to question God's love for us. We need to overcome these satanic assaults by finding and confessing the Bible verses that will silence our accuser. Here are some examples:

There is therefore now no condemnation for those who are in Christ Jesus. (Romans 8:1)

IN ORDER TO MAKE
THE RIGHT CONFESSION,
WE NEED TO UNDERSTAND THE
SCOPE OF SALVATION.

*But God demonstrates His own love toward us, in that while
we were yet sinners, Christ died for us.* (Romans 5:8)

*And we have come to know and have believed the love which
God has for us.* (1 John 4:16)

On the basis of these verses, I can make the following personal confession: "I am in Christ Jesus; therefore, I am not under condemnation. God proved His love for me by the fact that Christ died for me while I was still a sinner. I know and believe the love that God has for me." As I resist all negative feelings and maintain this positive, scriptural confession, condemnation and rejection are replaced in my experience by peace and acceptance.

Your need may be in the area of physical healing and health. Scripture tells us, concerning Jesus, *"He himself took our infirmities, and carried away our diseases"* (Matthew 8:17), and *"By His wounds you were healed"* (1 Peter 2:24). These statements provide the basis for the confession that is appropriate in this area. Every time sickness threatens me, instead of letting my mind dwell on the symptoms, I respond with a positive confession: "Jesus Himself took my infirmities and carried away my diseases, and by His wounds I was healed." At first I might waver, caught in the tension between the symptoms of my physical body and the unchanging truths of God's Word. But as I continue to confess God's truth, it becomes a part of me—just like the multiplication tables. Even if I wake up in the middle of the night with the symptoms of three different diseases in my body, my spirit can still make the right confession: "By His wounds I was healed."

If my need is in yet another area, then I make the confession that is appropriate to that area. For instance, if I am going through a period of financial shortage, I remind myself of 2 Corinthians 9:8: *"And God is able to make all grace abound to you, that always having all sufficiency in everything, you may have an abundance for every good deed."* I refuse to entertain my fears. I conquer fear by

SALVATION INCLUDES SPIRITUAL,
PHYSICAL, PSYCHOLOGICAL,
FINANCIAL, MATERIAL, AND
ETERNAL BENEFITS.

thanksgiving. I continue to thank God that the revealed level of His provision for me is abundance. As I maintain this confession, I see God intervene in such a way that the truth of His Word is made real in my financial situation.

Progressively—area by area, need by need, situation by situation—*"confession is made unto salvation"* (Romans 10:10 KJV). Each problem that we encounter becomes a stimulus to make the confession that declares God's answer to that problem. The more complete and consistent our confessions, the more fully we enter into the experiential enjoyment of our salvation.

THE HIGH PRIEST OF OUR CONFESSION

One major, distinctive theme throughout the epistle to the Hebrews is the high priesthood of Jesus Christ. As a high priest, Jesus ministers as our personal representative in the presence of God the Father. He covers us with His righteousness, offers up our prayers, presents our needs, and becomes the surety for the fulfillment of God's promises on our behalf. However, as we trace this theme of Christ's high priesthood through the epistle, we discover that it is invariably linked to our confession. The confession that we make on earth determines the extent to which Jesus is free to exercise His priestly ministry on our behalf in heaven.

In Hebrews 3:1, we are exhorted to consider Jesus Christ as the *"High Priest of our confession."* This links Christ's high priesthood directly to our confession. It is our confession that makes His priestly ministry effective on our behalf. Each time we make the right confession, we have the whole authority of Christ as our High Priest behind us. Again, He becomes the surety for the fulfillment of what we confess. But if we fail to make the right confession, or if we confess doubt or unbelief rather than faith, then we give Christ no opportunity to minister as our High Priest. Right confession invokes His priestly ministry on our behalf, but wrong confession shuts us off from it.

RIGHT CONFESSION LINKS
US TO GOD'S UNCHANGING
FAITHFULNESS, WISDOM, AND
POWER ON OUR BEHALF.

In Hebrews 4:14, the writer again linked the high priesthood of Jesus directly to our confession: *"Since then we have a great high priest who has passed through the heavens, Jesus the Son of God, let us hold fast our confession."* The emphasis here is on firmly holding on to our confession. Once we have brought the words of our mouths into agreement with God's written Word, we must be careful not to change or go back to a position of unbelief. Many pressures may come against us. It may seem that things are going precisely contrary to what we expected. All natural sources of help may fail. But by our faith and our confession, we must continue to hold on to the things that do not change: the Word of God and Jesus Christ as our High Priest at God's right hand.

In the tenth chapter of Hebrews, the writer stressed for the third time the connection between Christ's high priesthood and our confession:

> And since we have a great priest over the house of God, let us draw near with a sincere heart in full assurance of faith, having our hearts sprinkled clean from an evil conscience and our bodies washed with pure water. Let us hold fast the confession of our hope without wavering, for He who promised is faithful; and let us consider how to stimulate one another to love and good deeds. (Hebrews 10:21–24)

We see that the recognition of Jesus as our High Priest places upon us three successive obligations, each introduced by the words *"let us."* The first is related to God: *"Let us draw near with a sincere heart"* (verse 22). The second obligation concerns our own confession: *"Let us hold fast the confession of our hope without wavering"* (verse 23). The third obligation is related to our fellow believers: *"Let us consider how to stimulate one another to love and good deeds"* (verse 24). Central to our obligations to God and to our fellow believers is our obligation to ourselves: to firmly hold on to the right confession. The measure in which we do this will determine the measure in which we will be able to fulfill our obligations to God and to our fellow believers.

In the three passages of Hebrews that we have looked at, there is mounting emphasis on the importance of maintaining a right confession. In Hebrews 3:1, we are simply told that Jesus is the *"High Priest of our confession."* In Hebrews 4:14, we are exhorted to *"hold fast our confession."* In Hebrews 10:23, we are exhorted to hold fast our confession *"without wavering."* This increasing emphasis suggests that we are likely to be subjected to ever increasing pressures that would cause us to change or to weaken our confession. Many of us could testify that this is true in our experience. Therefore, the warning is timely. No matter what may be the pressures against us, victory comes only through firmly holding on to our confession.

In the last of these three exhortations in Hebrews, the writer gave us a specific reason for holding fast and not wavering. He said, *"For He who promised is faithful"* (Hebrews 10:23). Our confession links us to the High Priest who cannot change. Confession is the God-appointed means by which we invoke His faithfulness, His wisdom, and His power on our behalf.

SUMMARY

In God's plan of salvation, faith is linked directly to confession. Confession (or profession) means that we systematically make the words of our mouths agree with the written Word of God. This requires continual self-discipline. In each circumstance that confronts us, we must refuse to be swayed by our feelings or our senses; we must resolutely reaffirm what Scripture has to say about each situation. At first there may be struggle and tension, but ultimately the Word of God becomes indelibly imprinted on our hearts, and thereafter it flows out naturally through our mouths.

We must be careful that the practice of confession does not degenerate into a mere technique. The following are five practical safeguards:

1. We must begin by renouncing our own wills and submitting to God's will.

2. We must keep our confessions based strictly on Scripture.

3. We must be continually led by the Holy Spirit.

4. We must always rely on God's supernatural grace, never merely on our own natural abilities.

5. Where there is a conflict between our senses and God's Word, we must take the same stand that Abraham took: conditions revealed by our senses are *real*, but not *final*.

As we progressively apply the right confession to every area of our lives, we move forward into an ever fuller experience of salvation—that is, God's total provision obtained for us by the death of Christ.

Right confession links us directly to Christ as our High Priest. Right confession invokes His unchanging faithfulness, wisdom, and power on our behalf.

A FAITH-FILLED HEART IS THE
ONLY KIND OF HEART THAT IS
ACCEPTABLE TO GOD.

8

FAITH MUST BE WORKED OUT

We have seen that faith must be confessed with the mouth. But is that all? So often religious people are guilty of using empty words without real meaning. How can we avoid this? How can we be sure that the words we use in our confession really proceed from genuine faith in our hearts? Scripture gives a simple, practical answer to this question: Faith that is confessed with the mouth must be backed up by appropriate actions. *"Faith without works [that is, without appropriate actions] is dead"* (James 2:26).

FAITH WORKS BY LOVE

In Galatians 5:6, Paul went to the heart of the matter: *"For in Christ Jesus neither circumcision nor uncircumcision means anything, but faith working through love."* Paul here established four vital points that follow each other in logical order.

First, using circumcision as an example, Paul said that no outward ritual or ceremony can, by itself, commend us to God. God is primarily concerned with the internal, not the external.

Second, the one essential element in true Christianity is faith. A faith-filled heart is the only kind of heart that is acceptable to God. There is no substitute for it! In chapter five of this book,

I have already pointed out the Bible's insistent emphasis on the necessity and centrality of faith.

Third, Paul told us that faith works. The very nature of faith is to be active. Where there is no appropriate activity, there is no genuine faith.

Fourth, the way in which faith naturally acts is by love. Where there is no love manifested, there is no genuine faith. Love is essentially positive, strengthening, comforting, and edifying. Where actions are all negative, critical, and uncharitable, there is no evidence of love and therefore none of faith. Such actions may perhaps proceed from religion, but certainly not from faith.

One book of the New Testament that emphasizes the relationship between faith and works is the epistle of James. Some commentators suggest that there is a difference between James's view of faith and Paul's view of faith. They say that Paul emphasized salvation by faith alone, without works, while James asserted that faith must be expressed by works. Personally, I find no contradiction, only two opposite sides of the same truth. We are justified by faith without works, because there are no works we can do that will earn us righteousness. But once we are justified by faith without works, a valid faith will naturally express itself through works. So Paul told us *how* to receive righteousness from God, and James told us what results follow *when* we receive righteousness from God. I see no conflict between these two views, only a difference of emphasis.

Furthermore, it is completely wrong to suggest that Paul put no emphasis on works. In Galatians 5:6, as we have already seen, he showed that the very nature of faith is to work—and to work through love. He brought out the same truth in the famous thirteenth chapter of 1 Corinthians, known as the Love Chapter, and in many other places in his writings.

JAMES EMPHASIZED WORKS

The main part of James's teaching concerning faith and works is contained in chapter two of his epistle, verses fourteen through twenty-six. I will divide up this passage into six main sections and analyze each in order.

CONFESSION WITHOUT ACTION

What use is it, my brethren, if a man says he has faith, but he has no works? Can that faith save him? If a brother or sister is without clothing and in need of daily food, and one of you says to them, "Go in peace, be warmed and be filled," and yet you do not give them what is necessary for their body, what use is that? Even so faith, if it has no works, is dead, being by itself.

(James 2:14–17)

We need to see that James is describing a man who *says* he has faith. The man claims to have faith, but his behavior contradicts his claim. Confronted by a fellow believer in desperate physical need, this man merely offers words of comfort but does nothing practical to help. His failure to act in the appropriate way shows that his words of comfort are empty and insincere. The same principle applies to our profession, or confession, of faith. If it is not followed by appropriate actions, then all we have is a lifeless form of words, without any inner reality.

THEOLOGY VERSUS LIFE

But someone may well say, "You have faith, and I have works; show me your faith without the works, and I will show you my faith by my works." (James 2:18)

I always accept this verse as a personal challenge. Do I have a faith that is mere abstract theology, or do I demonstrate what I believe by what I do? The world has grown tired of faith presented

GOD LED ABRAHAM STEP-BY-STEP,
IN ONE ACT OF OBEDIENCE
AFTER ANOTHER, GRADUALLY
MATURING HIS FAITH.

as an abstract diagram; it is eager to see it in the form of a working model. My personal conviction is that a theology that does not work in practice is not valid.

THE DEVIL'S ORTHODOXY

> *Thou believest that there is one God; thou doest well: the devils also believe, and tremble.* (James 2:19 KJV)

It is highly orthodox to believe that there is only one true God. But this is not enough. Even the demons believe that—and shudder! I am convinced that the devil himself believes the whole Bible. He is much more orthodox than many theologians! What, then, is missing in faith such as this? The answer can be given in one word: *obedience*. Although Satan and his demons believe in one true God, they persist in their rebellion against Him. True faith leads to submission and obedience. Otherwise, our faith is in vain!

THE EXAMPLE OF ABRAHAM

> *But are you willing to recognize, you foolish fellow, that faith without works is useless? Was not Abraham our father justified by works, when he offered up Isaac his son on the altar? You see that faith was working with his works, and as a result of the works, faith was perfected; and the Scripture was fulfilled which says, "And Abraham believed God, and it was reckoned to him as righteousness," and he was called the friend of God. You see that a man is justified by works, and not by faith alone.* (James 2:20–24)

James next turned to the life of Abraham to illustrate his point. To follow what he was saying, we need to look at some of the main incidents in Abraham's life. In Genesis 11:31–12:7, God called Abraham to leave Ur of the Chaldeans in order to go to a land that he was to receive as an inheritance. When Abraham obeyed,

THREE THINGS MUST NEVER BE
SEPARATED FROM ONE ANOTHER:
FAITH, CONFESSION, AND
APPROPRIATE ACTION.

God led him to the land of Canaan. In Genesis 15, Abraham complained to God that he still had no heir, no son from his own body, to inherit the land. In reply, God showed him the stars at night and said, *"So shall your descendants be"* (verse 5). Abraham's response is recorded in Genesis 15:6: *"Then he believed in the Lord; and He reckoned it to him as righteousness."* At this point, God reckoned Abraham as being righteous, not on the basis of any good works he had done, but solely because he had believed God.

However, James pointed out that this was not the end of Abraham's faith relationship with God. Having believed God and having had righteousness reckoned to him on the basis of faith alone, Abraham then went on to work out his faith in a whole series of actions. In the next seven chapters of Genesis, we find that God led Abraham step-by-step, in one act of obedience after another, gradually maturing his faith over a period of about forty years. Finally, in Genesis 22, Abraham came to the point where he could face the supreme test of his faith: the offering up of his son Isaac on God's altar. Figuratively, Abraham did make the sacrifice, according to Hebrews 11:17–19. Although God did not ultimately require Abraham to sacrifice his son, Abraham was willing to do so, being fully persuaded that God would bring Isaac back to life again. Thus, he emerged triumphant from the test.

Abraham had not been ready to meet such a test in Genesis 15. It took many preparatory tests and struggles, many successive acts of obedience, to bring him to the point where he was willing to offer up Isaac. James explained this by saying that *"faith was working with his works, and as a result of the works, faith was perfected"* (James 2:22). Faith is always the starting point. There can be no other. Once faith has come into being, it is then worked out in successive tests. Faith responds to these tests with appropriate acts of obedience. Each act of obedience develops and strengthens faith and thus prepares it for the next test. Finally, through a whole

EACH ACT OF OBEDIENCE
DEVELOPS AND STRENGTHENS
FAITH AND THUS PREPARES IT FOR
THE NEXT TEST.

series of such tests and acts of obedience, faith is brought to maturity, or perfection.

THE EXAMPLE OF RAHAB

> And in the same way was not Rahab the harlot also justified by works, when she received the messengers and sent them out by another way? (James 2:25)

For his final example of the relationship between faith and works, James turned to Rahab. The story of Rahab is recorded in Joshua 2:1–22 and 6:21–25. One reason I enjoy her story is that it proves there is hope for the hopeless. Rahab was a sinful, heathen woman, living in Jericho, a city doomed by God to destruction. Yet, because of her faith, she escaped destruction, saved her entire household, was incorporated into God's people, and married a man who, together with her, is named as an ancestor of Jesus Christ. (See Matthew 1:5.)

Rahab's faith was not an empty profession; it was expressed by appropriate actions. The spies sent into Jericho by Joshua lodged in her house. When they were about to be captured, she risked her life to save them by hiding them on the roof. Before the spies left, Rahab struck a bargain with them, saying, in effect, "I have saved your lives. In return, I ask you to save me and my household." The spies agreed and pledged themselves to do what Rahab had asked. Actually, they made this pledge on behalf of God, rather than on their own behalf, since it was God Himself who brought about the destruction of Jericho by supernatural power. (See Joshua 6:1–5, 20.) With the bargain made, Rahab once again risked her life by letting the spies down through her window on a rope, since her house was on the city wall.

Before the spies left, they gave Rahab one final instruction: "If you want to be saved, tie this scarlet cord to your window. If the cord is not in the window, you will not be saved." The scarlet cord was a form of confession. By it, Rahab visibly showed her faith in the spies' promise. For us, in light of the New Testament, the scarlet cord beautifully represents our confession of faith in the blood of Christ.

Rahab's story vividly ties together faith, confession, and appropriate action. Rahab believed the spies' testimony that Jericho would be destroyed. She also believed their promise to save her and her household. But that was not enough. She had to confess her faith by placing the scarlet cord in the window. But that, too, was not enough. She had to act out her faith, even at the risk of her own life, by first hiding the spies on her roof and then letting them down from her window. It was appropriate that the scarlet cord was to be placed in that very window. The cord in the window would not have saved her if she had not also used the window to save the spies. Rahab's story illustrates three things that must never be separated from one another: faith, confession, and appropriate action.

JAMES'S CONCLUSION

> For just as the body without the spirit is dead, so also faith
> without works is dead. (James 2:26)

James concluded his analysis with a blunt but vivid analogy: faith without works is a corpse. It may be a mummy, solemnly preserved in a religious setting; nevertheless, it is dead. The only thing that can give life to a body is a spirit. Likewise, the only thing that can give life to faith is works, or appropriate actions.

FAITH IS A WALK

In the foregoing analysis, we saw how James used Abraham as his primary example of faith combined with works. In Romans, Paul also set Abraham before us as a pattern of faith that we should follow:

*And he received the sign of circumcision, a seal of the right-
eousness of the faith which he had while uncircumcised, that
he might be the father of all who believe without being circum-
cised, that righteousness might be reckoned to them, and the
father of circumcision to those who not only are of the circumcision, but who also follow in the steps of the faith of our father
Abraham which he had while uncircumcised.*

(Romans 4:11–12)

First, Paul explained that Abraham was not made righteous
by the act of circumcision. Rather, he received circumcision as an
outward seal of the righteousness already reckoned to him on the
basis of faith alone. The inference is that circumcision has no value
of its own; it must be based on faith.

Paul went on to say that Abraham, by his example of faith,
became the father of all subsequent believers, whether circum-
cised or uncircumcised. However, Paul laid down a condition that
we must all fulfill, regardless of racial or religious background, in
order to be Abraham's spiritual descendants. That condition is
that we "*follow in the steps of the faith of our father Abraham which
he had while uncircumcised*" (verse 12).

Paul spoke about "*the steps*" of Abraham's faith. This term presents a vivid picture, illustrating that faith is not static. It is not a
condition or a position. Rather, it is a progressive walk that we take
step-by-step. Each step springs out of our personal relationship
with God. For this reason, we cannot make all-embracing rules as
to how every believer should act. Different believers are in different stages of the faith walk. A believer who has been in the faith
many years should be further down the road than a new convert.
What God requires of a mature believer is different from what He
requires of a beginner. In my personal faith walk, I must take the
step that expresses my relationship with God at that moment. I
cannot take the same steps as other believers who are either more
or less mature than I am.

WHAT GOD REQUIRES OF A
MATURE BELIEVER IS DIFFERENT
FROM WHAT HE REQUIRES
OF A BEGINNER.

Faith, then, is a walk—the outcome of an ongoing, personal relationship between God and each believer. Every step in that walk is an act of obedience. Thus, as we walk in a right relationship with God, worked out in progressive acts of obedience, our faith is developed and finally brought to maturity.

SUMMARY

The confession of our faith must be accompanied by appropriate acts, motivated by love. Without these acts, our faith is in vain.

The epistle of James establishes three principles governing the relationship between faith and works: first, confession without action is worthless; second, theology must be made to work in practical living; and, third, orthodoxy must be accompanied by obedience.

James illustrated these principles by two Old Testament examples. The first example is Abraham. He had righteousness reckoned to him by God on the basis of faith alone. But, thereafter, his faith was developed and matured by progressive acts of obedience, culminating in his willingness to offer his son Isaac on God's altar. The second example is Rahab. She did not merely believe the spies' report; she risked her life to save them. She also confessed her faith in the spies' promise by hanging a scarlet cord in her window. Thus, she combined faith, confession, and appropriate action.

James concluded his analysis by declaring that faith without works is as lifeless as a body without a spirit.

Paul, in turn, used the example of Abraham to demonstrate that faith is not a static condition—but a progressive walk arising out of a personal relationship with God. Each step in this walk is an act of obedience. Through a whole series of such steps, faith is developed and finally brought to maturity.

WE ARE SPIRITUALLY MATURE
WHEN GOD IS THE SOURCE OF OUR
DEEPEST JOY AND THE OBJECT OF
OUR HIGHEST DEVOTION.

9

FAITH MUST BE TESTED

Faith, as we have learned, must be confessed with the mouth and must be worked out in action. Now we come to the third "must." This is the one we usually do not like to face. Nevertheless, we cannot avoid it: Faith must be tested.

EXULTING IN TRIBULATION

When Paul spoke of our faith relationship with God through Christ in Romans 5:1–11, he used the word *exult* three times. This is a very strong word denoting a confidence that actually causes us to boast.

In verse two, Paul said, *"We exult in hope of the glory of God."* This is not difficult to understand. If we really believe that we are even now heirs of God's glory and that we are going to share it with Him throughout eternity, it is natural to feel and to express excitement and joyful anticipation.

But in verse three, Paul used precisely the same word again. He said, *"And not only this, but we also exult in our tribulations…."* At first sight, this idea seems ridiculous. Who could ever imagine exulting in tribulations—in hardship, persecution, loneliness, misunderstanding, poverty, sickness, or bereavement? Why should Paul suggest, or God expect, that we should exult in such situations?

Fortunately, Paul gave us a reason:

> *...knowing that tribulation brings about perseverance; and perseverance, proven character; and proven character, hope; and hope does not disappoint, because the love of God has been poured out within our hearts through the Holy Spirit who was given to us.* (Romans 5:3–5)

To sum up Paul's answer, the reason for exulting even in tribulation is that, when tribulation is received as from God and endured in faith, it produces results in our character that cannot be produced any other way.

Analyzing Paul's answer, we find that he listed four successive stages in character development that result from meeting the test of tribulation. Let's examine each stage.

The first stage is *"perseverance"* (verses 3–4). This word could also be translated "endurance." Perseverance is an essential aspect of Christian character. Without it, we are not able to enter into many of God's choicest blessings and provisions for us.

The second stage is *"proven character"* (verse 4). The Greek word here is *dokime*. Some alternative translations of this word are as follows: *"strength of character"* (TLB); *"a mature character"* (PHILLIPS); *"proof that we have stood the test"* (NEB). The word *dokime* is closely associated with metal that has stood the test of the crucible—a picture to which we will return shortly.

The third stage is *"hope"* (verses 4–5). J. B. Phillips renders this *"a steady hope."* This hope is not mere daydreaming, wishful thinking, or flights of fancy that are an escape from reality. Hope of this kind is a strong, serene, confident expectation of good—the good that will ultimately result from the process of testing.

The fourth stage is *"the love of God [that] has been poured out within our hearts"* (verse 5), which, far from being a disappointment, greatly exceeds any hope we could ever have entertained. Thus, God's final objective in dealing with our character is to bring us into the enjoyment of His divine love.

Moving on to verse eleven, we come to Paul's third use of the word *exult*: *"And not only this, but we also exult in God through our Lord Jesus Christ."* Here again, we have a divine objective. God is not satisfied that our joy or our confidence should rest merely in what He has done for us—no matter how wonderful His blessings, His gifts, and His provisions may be. God's purpose is that we should find our final, and highest, satisfaction in nothing and no one but God Himself. This would not be possible without the process of character development already outlined. A sure mark of spiritual maturity is when God alone becomes both the source of our deepest joy and the object of our highest devotion.

It is interesting to compare Paul's teaching here in Romans 5 with his teaching in 1 Corinthians 13, the famous chapter on divine love. In Romans, Paul showed us that the way to enter into the fullness of divine love is by perseverance, or endurance. In 1 Corinthians 13, he put it the other way around. He told us that love is the only thing strong enough to endure every test: *"Love… bears all things, believes all things, hopes all things, endures all things"* (verses 4, 7). Scripture thus reveals there is a bond between love and endurance that cannot be severed.

In Romans 5, Paul presented faith, hope, and love as three successive phases of Christian experience: faith leads to hope, and hope leads to love. In 1 Corinthians 13:13, he presented these three qualities in the same order, but he emphasized that, while each is of permanent value, love is the greatest: *"But now abide faith, hope, love, these three; but the greatest of these is love."*

As we contemplate these three beautiful qualities in the mirror of God's Word, we need to keep the "eyes of our hearts" (see

Ephesians 1:18) fastened on them until they become an enduring part of our own characters. In this way, the truth of the following verse is worked out in our experience:

> *But we all, with unveiled face beholding as in a mirror the glory of the Lord, are being transformed into the same image from glory to glory, just as from the Lord, the Spirit.*
>
> (2 Corinthians 3:18)

"From glory to glory" means, at least in part, from faith to hope, and from hope to love.

In his epistle, James presented the same concept of faith being developed by testing:

> *Consider it all joy, my brethren, when you encounter various trials, knowing that the testing of your faith produces endurance. And let endurance have its perfect result, that you may be perfect and complete, lacking in nothing.* (James 1:2–4)

Paul told us that we are to exult in tribulations; James told us that we are to count all our trials joy. Both instructions are contrary to our natural thinking, but both have the same purpose. Testing—and testing alone—can produce endurance. And it is only through endurance that we can enter into the fullness of God's will for our lives. James expressed this truth by saying, *"That you may be perfect and complete, lacking in nothing."* With such an end as this in view, we have a logical reason to accept the testing of our faith joyfully.

TESTED BY FIRE

Like Paul and James, Peter also warned us of the trials that our faith must undergo. He described Christians as those *"who are protected by the power of God through faith for a salvation ready to be revealed in the last time"* (1 Peter 1:5). Peter emphasized that it is only through our faith that God's power can work effectively in our lives; therefore, continuing faith is a requirement for participating in the full and final revelations of God's salvation. Then, in the next two verses, he described how our faith will be tested:

> *In this* [the expectation of salvation] *you greatly rejoice, even though now for a little while, if necessary, you have been distressed by various trials, that the proof of your faith, being more precious than gold which is perishable, even though tested by fire, may be found to result in praise and glory and honor at the revelation of Jesus Christ.*

Here Peter compared the testing of our faith to the way gold was tested and purified at that time—by fire in a furnace. He returned to the same theme later on:

> *Beloved, do not be surprised at the fiery ordeal among you, which comes upon you for your testing, as though some strange thing were happening to you; but to the degree that you share the sufferings of Christ, keep on rejoicing.* (1 Peter 4:12–13)

At first, as we pass through *"the fiery ordeal,"* we may interpret it as *"some strange thing"*—something that does not belong to the Christian life. But Peter assured us that, on the contrary, testing of this kind is a necessary part of life. It is essential for the purifying of our faith, just as fire is essential for the purifying of gold. Therefore, he exhorted us to *"keep on rejoicing."* We find in the teaching of Peter, as we have found in that of Paul and James, the seeming paradox of intense testing associated with intense joy.

The prophet Malachi painted a vivid picture of Jesus, as the long-awaited Messiah, coming to His people and dealing with them as a refiner deals with gold and silver:

> *But who can endure the day of His coming?... For He is like a refiner's fire and like fullers' soap. And He will sit as a smelter*

IN THE TRIALS THROUGH WHICH
WE PASS, IT IS SPECIFICALLY OUR
FAITH THAT IS BEING TESTED.

and purifier of silver, and He will purify the sons of Levi and refine them like gold and silver, so that they may present to the LORD *offerings in righteousness.* (Malachi 3:2–3)

In purifying gold and silver, the refiner of Bible times put the metal in a melting pot over the hottest fire that he could produce. He usually built the fire in some form of a clay oven and used bellows to fan the flame. As the metal was heated in the pot, the dross—that is, the various impurities—was forced to the surface and was skimmed off by the refiner. (See Proverbs 25:4.) This process continued until all impurities had been removed and nothing but the pure metal was left.

It has been said that the refiner, bending over the metal in his pot, was not satisfied that it was completely pure until he could see his own image accurately reflected in its surface. In the same way, the Lord, who is our Refiner, continues to apply the fires of testing to us until He sees His own image reflected without distortion in our lives.

Trials or afflictions are the crucible in which God refines and purifies His people until they meet the requirements of His holiness. Various Old Testament prophets applied this picture very beautifully to the remnant of Israel, who are destined to survive God's judgments and be restored to His favor. For example, in Isaiah 48:10, God says to them, *"Behold, I have refined you, but not as silver; I have tested you in the furnace of affliction."*

Again, He says in the book of Zechariah,

And I will bring the third part through the fire, refine them as silver is refined, and test them as gold is tested. They will call on My name, and I will answer them; I will say, "They are My people," and they will say, "The LORD *is my God."*
(Zechariah 13:9)

Metals that pass the test of the furnace are called "refined"; these metals alone have a recognized value. Metals that fail to pass the test are called "rejected." In Jeremiah 6:30, Israel was called *"rejected silver"* because even the severe, repeated judgments of God had failed to purify them.

In the New Testament, Peter, James, and Paul all emphasized that, in the trials through which we pass, it is specifically our faith that is being tested. This is the metal of supreme value that cannot be accepted until it has passed the test of fire. At the Last Supper, Jesus warned Peter that he was soon going to deny his Lord. In this context, Jesus said to him, *"But I have prayed for you, that your faith may not fail"* (Luke 22:32). In view of the impending pressures and the weaknesses in Peter's own character, his failure in the hour of crisis was inevitable. Nothing could prevent that. But, even so, all would not be lost. A way would still be open for him to return and to confess his Lord once more, on one condition: that his faith did not fail.

The same is true for each of us. There will be times of pressure that will seem unendurable. It may be that, like Peter, we will yield and temporarily fail. But all is not lost! There is a way back, on one condition: that our faith does not fail. No wonder, then, that faith is called *"precious"*—infinitely more so than its material counterpart, the *"gold which is perishable"* (1 Peter 1:7). As long as we do not abandon our faith under pressure, we will be able to echo the words of Job in his hour of testing and apparent disaster: *"But He [God] knows the way I take; when He has tried me, I shall come forth as gold"* (Job 23:10).

TWO KINDS OF TESTS

In Matthew 13, the parable of the sower describes the response of four different kinds of people to the message of God's Word. The seed that fell by the roadside represents people who never received the message into their hearts at all. The seed that fell on good ground represents people who received the message into their hearts and, by faith and obedience, brought forth enduring fruit.

But, between these two groups, Jesus described two other types of people. They are represented by the seed that fell on rocky places and the seed that fell among thorns. People in these two groups received the message into their hearts but later failed to meet the conditions for producing good, enduring fruit. Therefore, we may say of both groups that they failed to pass the tests to which they were subjected after receiving God's Word.

What kind of test is represented by each of these two groups? Let us look first at the seed that fell on rocky places. Jesus said this about the person represented by the rocky soil:

> *And the one on whom seed was sown on the rocky places, this is the man who hears the word, and immediately receives it with joy; yet he has no firm root in himself, but is only temporary, and when affliction or persecution arises because of the word, immediately he falls away.*　　(Matthew 13:20–21)

The exact words that Jesus used here are significant. He did not say, "*If* affliction or persecution arises," but "**When** *affliction or persecution arises.*" In other words, at some time or other, affliction and persecution are sure to come to everyone who receives God's Word. The question for each of us is not whether we will have to face these things, but whether our characters will have been so formed that we will come through them victorious, with our faith intact. For this to happen, we must allow God's Word to penetrate into the depths of our hearts, bringing everything into line with His will. There must be no *"rocky places"* anywhere within us to resist the application of the Word to our lives.

What about the seed that fell among thorns? Jesus said this about the person represented by the thorny soil:

> *And the one on whom seed was sown among the thorns, this is the man who hears the word, and the worry of the world,*

TESTING TAKES TWO MAIN FORMS:
WHEN THINGS ARE TOO HARD AND
WHEN THINGS ARE TOO EASY.

and the deceitfulness of riches choke the word, and it becomes unfruitful. (Matthew 13:22)

The test that eliminates people of this type is not affliction or persecution. On the contrary, it is just the opposite: worldly cares and riches. The pressures of human popularity and materialistic success choke out the truth of God that such people have received. In the end, God's truth has no effect on their lives. Instead of being transformed into the likeness of Christ, they become conformed to the unbelieving, Christ-rejecting world around them.

Very simply, we may say that these two groups represent the two types of tests to which all believers may expect to be subjected. The first test comes when things are too hard. The second test comes when things are too easy. Some people give way under the pressure of persecution; others give way under the pressure of materialistic success. In the book of Proverbs, there are verses for both types of people. To those who yield under persecution, Solomon said, *"If thou faint in the day of adversity, thy strength is small"* (Proverbs 24:10 KJV). To those who are led away by success, Solomon said, *"For the turning away [my Bible's margin says "ease"] of the simple shall slay them, and the prosperity of fools shall destroy them"* (Proverbs 1:32 KJV). Tragically enough, Solomon himself belonged to this latter category. In spite of all his God-given wisdom, in the end, his prosperity made a fool of him and destroyed him.

On the other hand, we see in Moses a man who endured both of these tests. For forty years, he enjoyed the wealth and luxury of the Egyptian court, being the probable heir to Pharaoh's throne. But then, when he came to maturity, he turned his back on all that luxury and chose the path of loneliness and apparent failure. This is vividly described in the book of Hebrews:

By faith Moses, when he had grown up, refused to be called the son of Pharaoh's daughter; choosing rather to endure

JESUS IS SET BEFORE US AS OUR
FINAL, PERFECT PATTERN OF
ENDURANCE AND ULTIMATE VICTORY.

ill-treatment with the people of God, than to enjoy the passing
pleasures of sin. (Hebrews 11:24–25)

For the next forty years, Moses underwent the affliction test. He was an exile from his people, a nonentity in the eyes of the world, tending a flock of sheep for his father-in-law on the farthest edge of a barren wilderness.

Yet, when Moses had finally passed both of these tests, at the age of eighty he emerged as the God-appointed deliverer and leader of his people. What a striking example of the words I quoted earlier from James 1:4: *"Let endurance have its perfect result, that you may be perfect and complete, lacking in nothing."*

THE TWO IMPOSTORS

In his famous poem entitled "If," Rudyard Kipling said something penetratingly true concerning success and failure:

If you can meet with Triumph and Disaster,
    And treat those two impostors just the same…

Whether we say "Triumph and Disaster" or "Success and Failure," Kipling's description is correct—they are both impostors. Neither of them is what it seems to be; neither is permanent.

Fortunately, we have been given a perfect example of how to deal with these two impostors. No one ever met them more fully or exposed their pretentious claims more effectively than Jesus Himself. He experienced moments of unparalleled success, as when the whole multitude cast their garments in the road before Him and welcomed Him as God's prophet into Jerusalem. Likewise, He experienced moments of total failure, as when, one week later, the same multitude cried out, "Crucify Him! Crucify Him!" Even His closest friends and followers forsook Him. Yet Jesus was never unduly elated by success or cast down by failure. Through both alike, He was motivated by one supreme purpose:

to do His Father's will and to finish the work His Father had given Him to do. (See, for example, John 4:34.) This purpose, unswervingly pursued, carried Him victoriously through both kinds of tests—success and failure.

In the twelfth chapter of Hebrews, the writer first challenged us by mentioning the Old Testament believers whose faith overcame every kind of test, and then he set Jesus before our eyes as the final, perfect pattern of endurance and ultimate victory:

> *Therefore, since we have so great a cloud of witnesses surrounding us, let us also lay aside every encumbrance, and the sin which so easily entangles us, and let us run with endurance the race that is set before us, fixing our eyes on Jesus, the author and perfecter of faith, who for the joy set before Him endured the cross, despising the shame, and has sat down at the right hand of the throne of God.* (Hebrews 12:1–2)

As we follow this exhortation and make Jesus our pattern, we discover that He is, in truth, both *"the author and perfecter of* [our] *faith."* He who began the work in each of us by His grace will likewise complete it by His grace. (See Philippians 1:6.) His victory became the guarantee of ours. All He requires is that we keep our eyes fixed on Him.

SUMMARY

Scripture clearly warns us that our faith will be subjected to severe tests. These are necessary to prove its genuineness and to develop strong Christian character in us.

Paul listed four results of such testing: first, perseverance (or endurance); second, proven character; third, hope (a strong, serene, confident expectation of good); and, fourth, God's love filling our hearts. Finally, testing brings us into a relationship with God in which we find our highest satisfaction in nothing and in no one but Him.

James and Peter likewise taught that tribulation is a necessary part of our total Christian experience. Peter compared the tests we undergo to the fire used by the refiner to purify gold and give it the highest possible value. This word picture was also used by the Old Testament prophets to describe God's dealings with Israel.

Paul, James, and Peter all assured us emphatically that once we understand the purpose for our tribulations, we will embrace them with joy. Even if we fail temporarily under extreme pressure, we must never give up our faith.

Testing takes two main forms: when things are too hard and when things are too easy. Moses is an example of a man who endured both of these tests and finally emerged as the God-appointed leader of his people. However, the supreme example of dealing with both success and failure is Jesus Himself. As we follow His example, He brings our faith to full maturity.

OFFERING OUR BODIES TO GOD AS
A LIVING SACRIFICE REPRESENTS A
TOTAL SURRENDER TO HIM.

10

THE MEASURE OF FAITH

A practical study of the Christian's faith must also take into account the teaching of Paul on "the measure of faith":

> I urge you therefore, brethren, by the mercies of God, to present your bodies a living and holy sacrifice, acceptable to God, which is your spiritual [or, logical] service of worship. And do not be conformed to this world, but be transformed by the renewing of your mind, that you may prove what the will of God is, that which is good and acceptable and perfect. For through the grace given to me I say to every man among you not to think more highly of himself than he ought to think; but to think so as to have sound judgment, as God has allotted to each a measure of faith. For just as we have many members in one body and all the members do not have the same function, so we, who are many, are one body in Christ, and individually members one of another. And since we have gifts that differ according to the grace given to us, let each exercise them accordingly: if prophecy, according to the proportion of his faith; if service, in his serving; or he who teaches, in his teaching; or he who exhorts, in his exhortation; he who gives, with liberality; he who leads, with diligence; he who shows mercy, with cheerfulness.
>
> (Romans 12:1–8)

Paul opened the twelfth chapter of Romans with the words, "*I urge you therefore.*" Someone has remarked that when we come across a "therefore" in the Bible, we need to find out what it is there for! In this case, the "*therefore*" refers back to all that Paul had been saying in the previous eleven chapters of Romans. In chapters one through eight, he explained how Christ, through His death on the cross, made a complete and final atonement for sin and all its evil consequences. In chapters nine through eleven, he dealt with the stubbornness and blindness of Israel, God's people under the old covenant, and with the infinite grace and forbearance that God continued to show toward them.

Having thus unfolded God's mercy toward both Jew and Gentile, Paul said, "*Therefore…*" (verse 1). In light of all that God has done for all of us, what is our "*spiritual* [or, logical, as it says in my Bible's margin] *service*" (verse 1)? What is the very least that God can ask of us? It is that we offer Him our "*bodies* [as] *a living and holy sacrifice*" (verse 1)—that we lay ourselves totally and without reserve on God's altar. When Paul spoke of a living sacrifice, he was contrasting our sacrifice with the sacrifices made under the old covenant. In those sacrifices, the body of the animal was first killed, then placed on the altar. Under the new covenant, each one of us is required to place his body just as totally and finally at God's disposal—but with one difference: our bodies are not killed; we remain to serve God in life rather than by death.

This offering of our bodies to God as a living sacrifice represents a total surrender to Him. It opens up the way to a series of steps that lead us into the very center of God's will and provision. The first step is that we begin to change our whole lifestyle. We cease to be "*conformed to this world*" (Romans 12:2). We are "*transformed*" (verse 2). This transformation does not proceed from a set of rules governing our external conduct in matters such as food, dress, entertainment, and so on. It originates from an inner change in our minds. We are renewed in our minds. (See verse 2.) Our whole range of attitudes, values, and priorities is adjusted.

Earlier in Romans, Paul told us that *"the carnal mind is enmity against God: for it is not subject to the law of God"* (Romans 8:7 KJV). The term *"carnal mind"* refers to the way that it has become natural for all of us to think as a result of our sin and rebellion. This mind is actually at enmity with God. In human relationships, a person never reveals to an enemy what is important or precious to him. The same is true of God. As long as our minds remain at enmity with Him, there are many precious and wonderful things He will not reveal to us. But once our minds are reconciled to God by an act of surrender, they are no longer at enmity with Him but become progressively renewed by the Holy Spirit.

To our renewed minds, God can begin to reveal His will—the special plan He has for each one of us. God's will is unfolded in three successive phases as our minds become more and more renewed. In the first phase, God's will is *"good"* (Romans 12:2). We discover that He wants only what is good for us. In the second phase, God's will is *"acceptable"* (verse 2). The better we understand it, the more ready we are to accept it. In the third phase, God's will is *"perfect"* (verse 2). It is complete and all-embracing, making total provision for every area of our lives.

With our minds thus renewed, we do not *"think more highly of [ourselves] than [we] ought to think"* (verse 3). We cease to be proud, self-seeking, and self-assertive. We no longer are open to flights of fancy and self-deception. We become sober and realistic; we cultivate *"sound judgment"* (verse 3). We begin to assimilate the mind of Jesus, who said to the Father, *"Not My will, but Thine be done"* (Luke 22:42). God's plans and purposes are now more important to us than our own.

This leads us to the next discovery: God has given to each one of us a specific *"measure of faith"* (Romans 12:3). It is not for us to determine how much faith we should have. God has already

IN THE BODY OF CHRIST, EACH ONE
OF US IS A PARTICULAR MEMBER,
WITH A SPECIFIC PLACE AND A
SPECIFIC FUNCTION.

measured this for us and allotted to each of us the amount that we need. But what standard does God use to measure how much faith we need?

Paul's answer was to explain how the body of Christ functions:

For just as we have many members in one body and all the members do not have the same function, so we, who are many, are one body in Christ, and individually members one of another. (Romans 12:4–5)

As Christians, together we make up one complete body. Each one of us is a particular member of the body, with a specific place and a specific function. One is a "nose," another is an "ear." One is a "hand," another is a "foot," and so on.

In 1 Corinthians 12:12–28, Paul dealt more fully with the concept of the body and its members. He said that it is God who "*has placed the members, each one of them, in the body, just as He desired*" (verse 18). None of us can choose his own place or function in the body. All we can do is find and fill the place that God has appointed to us. As we have seen, doing this requires a renewed mind.

Paul went on to point out that, as members of one body, we are all interdependent. We need each other. None of us is free to do just as he pleases without regard to the other members. "*And the eye cannot say to the hand, 'I have no need of you'; or again the head to the feet, 'I have no need of you'*" (verse 21). The head is the highest member, typifying Christ Himself. (See Ephesians 4:15.) The feet are the lowest members, at the opposite end of the body. Yet the head needs the feet and cannot do without them. In light of this fact, we see more clearly why Paul said that in order to find our places in the body, we must not think too highly of ourselves but must learn to be sober and realistic.

This picture of the body and its members enables us to understand what Paul meant by the "*measure of faith*" (Romans 12:3).

Each of us is a member in the body with a specific function. To fulfill our functions, we need specific measures of faith. The type and amount of faith needed by each member vary. An eye needs "eye faith." A hand needs "hand faith." A foot needs "foot faith." This measure of faith is not interchangeable. The faith that enables a hand to function will not do for a foot. The faith that enables an eye to function will not do for an ear. Each member must have its own appropriate and specific measure of faith.

Once we have found our appointed places in the body and are functioning there with our appointed measures of faith, we are ready for the next phase of God's provision for us—His gifts (or, in the Greek, *charismata*). *"And since we have gifts that differ according to the grace given to us, let each exercise them accordingly: if prophecy, according to the proportion of his faith"* (Romans 12:6). In addition to prophecy, Paul named six other gifts: service, teaching, exhorting, giving, leading, and showing mercy. This is by no means an exhaustive list of all possible gifts but simply a selection to show the variety that is available.

An important principle is established here: Placement and function in the body come before gifts. Many Christians are overly preoccupied with gifts and ministries. They fasten their minds on certain gifts of their own choosing. Usually, these tend to be somewhat spectacular, such as gifts of healings or workings of miracles, or the ministry of an apostle or an evangelist. It is true that in 1 Corinthians 12:31, Paul told us to *"earnestly desire the greater gifts."* But it is significant that he did not tell us which are *"the greater gifts."* There is no absolute standard. The value of the gift is relative to our place in the body. The gifts that enable me to fulfill my God-appointed function are, for me, *"the greater gifts."*

Christians who are overly preoccupied with exciting or spectacular gifts have not heeded Paul's warning to cultivate *"sound judgment"* (Romans 12:3). Our first responsibility is not to decide what gifts we would like to have; it is to find our place in the body of Christ. This, in turn, will determine the type of gifts we will need in order to function there effectively. Experience indicates that once a Christian has settled the question of place and function, the needed gifts come into operation almost spontaneously, without undue effort or striving.

We may now summarize Paul's teaching in Romans 12:1–8. God has shown unfathomable grace and mercy to each of us through Christ. In order to fulfill our logical response to such grace and mercy, it is necessary that we go through the following successive steps:

1. We first present our bodies as a living sacrifice to God.

2. Through this act of surrender, our minds become progressively renewed by the Holy Spirit.

3. As the outward expression of this change in our minds, our whole lifestyle begins to change—we are transformed!

4. With our renewed minds, we are able to find out the will of God for our lives on three ascending levels: first, "*good*"; second, "*acceptable*"; third, "*perfect*" (Romans 12:2).

5. God's will, proved in experience, fits us into our appointed places as members in the body of Christ and enables us to function there.

6. We thus discover that God has given to each of us a measure of faith, exactly proportioned to our places and functions in the body. He gives a person "ear faith" if he is an ear, and "eye faith" if he is an eye.

7. As we function in our appointed places with our appointed measures of faith, the gifts that we need come into operation.

AS OUR ABILITY TO FUNCTION
EFFECTIVELY IN THE BODY GROWS,
OUR FAITH GROWS IN PROPORTION.

In chapter six of this book, we examined Paul's statement in Romans 10:17 that *"faith cometh by hearing, and hearing by the word of God"* (KJV). How does this truth relate to Paul's teaching in Romans 12:3–5 that God has allotted to each of us a specific measure of faith, directly related to our appointed places and functions in the body of Christ?

The answer, I believe, is this: Hearing serves a Christian in the same way that radar serves an airplane. The more sensitive we become to the radar of God's *rhema*—the special word that He speaks to each of us personally—the more surely and easily we will be guided to our appointed places and functions in the body of Christ. Finding our places is like the airplane landing accurately on the runway. Hearing is the radar that brings us in exactly where God wants us. Thereafter, as we continue to hear each new *rhema* that comes to us from God, we are enabled to stay in our places and to function there effectively.

The fact that God has allotted to each of us a specific measure of faith should not be taken to imply that our faith remains static. On the contrary, as our ability to function effectively in the body grows, our faith grows in proportion. More effective function requires increased faith. Conversely, increased faith produces more effective function. However, there is always a fixed relationship between faith and function.

Faith is not a commodity that we can buy or barter in the marketplaces of religion. Rather, it is the expression of a relationship with God, the outcome of an act of surrender that brings us into harmony with God's plan for our lives. As we continue in submission and obedience to God, our faith enables us to take the places and fulfill the functions God has ordained for us. This faith is extremely personal; a specific measure is allotted to each one of us. "My" faith will not work for you; "your" faith will not work for me. Each of us must have his own measure of faith, which fits his individual function in the body.

THE FAITH THAT GOD GIVES US IS
IN PROPORTION TO THE TASKS HE
ASKS US TO PERFORM.

While I was still a fairly young Christian, I remember being tremendously impressed by the faith I saw demonstrated in the life of a more mature believer, one who had made great sacrifices for the Lord and had achieved great success. Almost without thinking, I said one day, "Lord, I don't believe that I could ever have faith like that." Unexpectedly, the Lord gave me a clear, practical answer: "You can't have faith like that because you don't need it! I have not asked you to do what that other person has done." Ever since, I have been grateful for the lesson I learned at the time: The faith that God gives is in proportion to the tasks He asks us to perform.

Later in my ministry, I came across many Christians who obviously had not learned this lesson. They were constantly pleading and struggling for faith, yet they never seemed to have enough. There was an obvious lack of harmony between their faith and what they were seeking to do. I became convinced that it was not that God had not given them enough faith; it was that their faith was being misdirected. They were applying it to a task of their own choosing, not to the task that God had actually appointed for them.

Imagine a foot trying to function with a glove on, or a hand with a shoe on. Obviously, neither will work properly. There may not necessarily be anything wrong with any of the four things involved: the foot, the hand, the glove, and the shoe. Individually, each may be good and workable. But they are wrongly related to one another. A hand that puts on a shoe and wants to do the work of a foot will be awkward and unsuccessful, as will a foot that puts on a glove and tries to act like a hand. But when the hand puts on the glove and the foot puts on the shoe, harmony is restored, and success is achieved. So it is with the faith that God gives. It fits the member whom He appoints, as a glove fits a hand or a shoe fits a foot.

In Hebrews 4, the writer spoke about believers entering into their inheritance: *"For we who have believed enter that rest"* (verse 3).

Faith should bring us into rest. Once we have found our place in our God-given inheritance, we should know a deep, untroubled peace within. There may be much hard work, much pressure and opposition, but in the midst of it all, there is inward rest. Continual effort and striving almost certainly indicate that we have not yet found our God-appointed places and functions. We are still fumbling, like a hand in a shoe, or stumbling, like a foot in a glove.

A little further on in chapter four of Hebrews, the writer said, *"Let us therefore be diligent to enter that rest"* (verse 11). Diligence is required. There is no room for laziness or indifference in the Christian life. But we need to understand the goal to which our diligence should be directed. We are not exhorted, primarily, to acquire faith. We are exhorted to find our place in our inheritance, the very place in the body for which God has appointed us. Once we have succeeded in finding this place, we will be able to function there without continued struggle or effort—as easily as a foot walks or a hand handles.

SUMMARY

Effective Christian service begins with an act of surrender, whereby we present our bodies to God as a living sacrifice. This, in turn, leads to a change in our whole way of thinking. Our minds are renewed. Our total range of attitudes, values, and priorities is progressively adjusted. God's plans and purposes take precedence over our own.

With a renewed mind, we are able to see ourselves and other Christians as being individual members of one body. Our first priority is to find the place and fulfill the function in that body that God has appointed for us. As we succeed in this, we discover that God has allotted to each of us individually the measure of faith that our place and function require.

Functioning this way, with our appointed faith in our appointed place, we become open to the exercise of the particular gifts (or, *charismata*) that are most needed. These are, for us, the greater gifts.

If, however, we are continually striving after faith or gifts, this is usually an indication that we have not yet found our appointed place in the body. Once we have found our place, there is God-given harmony between our function, our faith, and our gifts.

GOD'S CREATIVE ABILITY
PROCEEDS OUT OF HIS FAITH. ALL
THAT HE DOES, HE DOES BY FAITH.

11

FAITH UNDOES THE FALL

In this closing chapter, we will approach the subject of faith from still another angle. We will see that biblical faith, as God imparts it and as it works in our lives, undoes the effects of the fall.

Scripture reveals that man was created in perfection but fell from that condition by a transgression, for which he was accountable to God. However, God was not content to leave man in his fallen condition. Rather, from that point onward, Scripture unfolds a magnificent theme of redemption. It is the story of how God buys man back for Himself by the death of Christ on the cross—and how He works out man's restoration, changing his nature and his ways to bring him back into God's original purpose. The key to this process of restoration is faith. In other words, the redemptive effect of exercising faith is that of reversing the results of the fall.

FAITH, SPEECH, AND CREATIVITY

To understand how faith reverses the fall, we must consider the nature of man, the steps that led to his fall, and the essence of the temptation to which he yielded. The original picture of man as God created him is found in Genesis 1:26: *"Then God said, 'Let Us make man in Our image, according to Our likeness.'"* As we follow this theme through Scripture, we discover that the *"likeness"* between God and man has various aspects.

Here we will concentrate on one aspect of the divine nature. It is seldom mentioned, but it is extremely significant. This aspect of God's nature, which has its counterpart in the nature of man, is the ability to exercise faith. As I mentioned briefly earlier in this book, faith is a part of God's own eternal nature. His creative ability proceeds out of His faith. All that He does, He does by faith. Furthermore, His faith finds its expression in the words that He speaks. His words are the channels of His faith and are therefore the instruments of His creative ability.

The effective power of God's faith in His own words is forcefully expressed in Ezekiel 12:25, where the Lord declared, *"For I the LORD shall speak, and whatever word I speak will be performed."* The introductory words *"I the LORD"* indicate that what follows is part of the eternal, unchanging nature of God. When God says something, it happens. Such is His faith in His own words.

There is a feature of the Hebrew language that vividly illustrates this fact about God and His words. Old Testament Hebrew contains one word, *dabar*, that can be translated equally well as "word" or "thing." Only the context indicates which translation is preferable. Often both are implied. This helps us to understand that God's words are *things*. When God speaks a word with His faith, that *word* becomes a *thing*.

In chapter six of this book, we saw that the same is also true of the Greek word *rhema*, used in the New Testament. God's *rhema*—His spoken word proceeding out of His faith—contains within it the power to fulfill whatever is spoken.

In Hebrews 11:3, we are told that the whole universe was brought into being by the creative power of God's faith in His own words: *"By faith we perceive that the universe was fashioned by the word of God, so that the visible came forth from the invisible*" (NEB). Behind the entire visible universe, faith discerns one supreme, originating cause that is invisible—"*the word of God.*" Thus, human faith recognizes the outworking of divine faith.

In chapter three of this book, dealing with the gift of faith, I referred to Psalm 33, where David graphically depicted this process of creation by the spoken word of God:

> *By the word of the* LORD *the heavens were made, and by the breath of His mouth all their host.... For He spoke, and it was done; He commanded, and it stood fast.*   (Psalm 33:6, 9)

In Genesis 1:3, we are given a specific example of how this process worked: "*Then God said, 'Let there be light'; and there was light.*" When God spoke the word "*light,*" the thing "light" was manifested. God's spoken word came forth as a thing.

Thus, we arrive at three conclusions about faith that help us to understand its unique power and importance. First, faith is part of the eternal nature of God. Second, faith is the creative power by which God brought the universe into being. Third, God's faith is expressed and made effective by the words that He speaks.

Because God created man with the ability to exercise faith, we find also in man the other two abilities that are related to faith: the ability to create and the ability to speak. It is significant that both of these abilities man shares with God also distinguish man from the animals.

By his very nature, man has creative ability. He can envision something that has never actually existed; then he can plan it and bring it into being. This distinguishes him from all known animals. A bird, for example, can build a marvelously complex nest, but it does so by instinct. A bird cannot envision something that has never existed, plan it, and bring it into being. Man can. In this sense, man is continually creating.

GOD'S FAITH IS EXPRESSED
AND MADE EFFECTIVE BY THE
WORDS HE SPEAKS.

Linked to man's creative ability is man's ability to speak. Without this ability, man would never be able to express his creative purposes. Man's capacity for intelligent, articulate speech is not shared by any known animals. It is a distinctive aspect of man's likeness to God.

From this, we see that man, as originally created, shares three related aspects of God's own nature: the ability to exercise faith, the ability to create, and the ability to speak.

SATAN'S ASSAULT ON FAITH

Because God has shared with man His ability to exercise faith, He requires him to use it. Consequently, when God created man, He placed him in a situation where faith was needed. Scripture makes it clear that God, as a person, did not remain permanently present with Adam in the garden. Instead, He left him with a substitute for His personal presence—His word. In chapter one of this book, we saw that faith connects us to two invisible realities—God and His Word. This was the type of relationship in which Adam found himself. He had been in direct personal contact with God, but when God was no longer present as a person in the garden, Adam was obligated to relate to God through the word that He had left him.

This word is recorded in the beginning of the book of Genesis:

> *Then the LORD God took the man and put him into the garden of Eden to cultivate it and keep it. And the LORD God commanded the man, saying, "From any tree of the garden you may eat freely; but from the tree of the knowledge of good and evil you shall not eat, for in the day that you eat from it you shall surely die."* (Genesis 2:15–17)

Verses sixteen and seventeen contain the words that God actually spoke to Adam. They fall into three sections: first, a

IF WE EVER LOSE FAITH IN GOD AS A
PERSON, WE WILL EVENTUALLY GIVE UP
OUR FAITH IN HIS WORD.

permission; second, a prohibition; and, third, a warning. The permission was this: *"From any tree of the garden you may eat freely"* (verse 16). The prohibition was this: *"But from the tree of the knowledge of good and evil you shall not eat"* (verse 17). Finally, the warning was this: *"For in the day that you eat from it you shall surely die"* (verse 17). That was God's threefold word to Adam: permission, prohibition, and warning.

As long as Adam remained rightly related to God through His word, he was blessed and secure. Satan could not touch him. But Satan was determined to alienate man from God and deprive him of His blessings. With characteristic craftiness, he did not begin by directly challenging Adam's relationship with God. Rather, he sought to undermine God's word to Adam. Furthermore, he approached Adam through the "weaker vessel," Eve. (See 1 Peter 3:7.)

The initial encounter between Satan and Eve is described in the third chapter of Genesis:

> *Now the serpent was more crafty than any beast of the field which the LORD God had made. And he said to the woman, "Indeed, has God said, 'You shall not eat from any tree of the garden'?" And the woman said to the serpent, "From the fruit of the trees of the garden we may eat; but from the fruit of the tree which is in the middle of the garden, God has said, 'You shall not eat from it or touch it, lest you die.'"*
>
> (Genesis 3:1–3)

In his strategy to deceive Eve, Satan did not begin by directly denying the word of God—that would have been too obvious! He began by merely questioning it. *"Indeed, has God said…?"* I believe Eve lost the battle the moment she entertained that question. If we are to retain a right relationship with God, there are some questions to which we must simply close our minds. But Eve trusted in her own judgment. She felt she had the ability to match that charming, intelligent serpent who had approached her in the garden. The root of her error was self-confidence.

The next stage of Satan's strategy is recorded in Genesis 3:4: *"And the serpent said to the woman, 'You surely shall not die!'"* Having first entertained the question, Eve no longer had the power to resist temptation.

However, Satan's strategy was not yet complete. To understand his final objective, we need to remind ourselves of two conclusions we reached in chapter five of this book. First, the ultimate object of true faith is God Himself. If we ever lose faith in God as a person, we will eventually give up our faith in His Word. Also, the opposite can happen: If we lose faith in God's Word, we will lose faith in God, as we will see in Eve's case. Second, if we always were to have unquestioning faith in God's goodness, God's wisdom, and God's power to provide, there would never be any motive to sin.

Satan operated according to these principles. By this time, he had succeeded in undermining Eve's faith in God's word. Now he went on to undermine her faith in God Himself. He achieved this by saying, *"For God knows that in the day you eat from it your eyes will be opened, and you will be like God, knowing good and evil"* (Genesis 3:5).

Taken in their context, Satan's words were aimed at discrediting God's motives in His dealings with Adam and Eve. He insinuated that God was an arbitrary despot, seeking to keep them in a state of unmerited inferiority through their ignorance. We might paraphrase Satan's charge against God as follows: "Do you really think that God loves you? Do you think He wants to fellowship with you? No! Don't you know He's just got you in this garden to keep you under His control? You're really not much better off than slaves. Now, if you were to eat of that tree, things would be different! You wouldn't have to depend on God any longer; you'd be just like God."

This was the final persuasion that broke Eve's relationship with God. She had already given up her confidence in God's word. Now she gave up her confidence in God Himself. Instead of seeing, all around her, the visible evidence of the love and goodness of the God whom she could not see, she began to accept Satan's dark, cynical picture of God. It was a picture of Him as an arbitrary tyrant whose purpose was to keep her and her husband in a state of inferiority, far below their real potential. She believed Satan's lie that, through eating from the forbidden tree, their innate potential for equality with God would be instantly released! She reasoned, "Could there be any higher motive than the desire to be like God?"

Eve's capitulation is recorded in chapter three of Genesis:

When the woman saw that the tree was good for food, and that it was a delight to the eyes, and that the tree was desirable to make one wise, she took from its fruit and ate; and she gave also to her husband with her, and he ate. (verse 6)

The key word here is *"saw."* Eve *"saw that the tree...."* The word indicates a transition from one realm to another. At this point, Eve abandoned her faith in the invisible realm of God and His word. Instead, she was moved by what she saw. She began to rely on her physical senses. She came down from the realm of faith to the realm of the senses.

THE NATURE OF TEMPTATION

In this lower realm, Eve was attracted to three features of the tree: it was good for food; it was a delight to the eyes; and it was desirable to make one wise. These features correspond to the basic forms of temptation listed by the apostle John in the New Testament:

Do not love the world, nor the things in the world. If anyone loves the world, the love of the Father is not in him. For all that

ADAM SUCCUMBED TO HIS TEMPTATION
BY EATING; JESUS OVERCAME HIS
TEMPTATION BY FASTING.

is in the world, the lust of the flesh and the lust of the eyes and
the boastful pride of life, is not from the Father, but is from the
world.   (1 John 2:15–16)

The sensual world, in God's terminology, is made up of three elements: *"the lust of the flesh and the lust of the eyes and the boastful pride of life."* In Scripture, the word *lust* usually denotes a strong desire that has become perverted and harmful. It does not submit to God's standards of righteousness. The first two forms of temptation listed here are lustful desires that affect man through his physical senses. The third form of temptation appeals to man's ego, or soul. The *"boastful pride of life"* is that inner urge in man that refuses to acknowledge his dependence on God but seeks to exalt himself. It finds expression in such statements as, "I can manage my own life. I don't need to depend on God. Why should I be inferior?"

When Jesus was in the wilderness, He was confronted by Satan with each of these three temptations. (See, for example, Luke 4:1–13.) Satan tempted Him to turn stones into bread—*"the lust of the flesh."* Then he showed Him all the kingdoms of the world with their power and glory—*"the lust of the eyes."* Finally, Satan tempted Jesus to cast Himself down from the pinnacle of the temple, thus performing a miracle on His own initiative that would glorify Himself, without submitting to the Father's will or seeking the Father's glory. That represented *"the boastful pride of life."*

There are some interesting comparisons between the temptation of Adam and the temptation of Jesus (who is called *"the last Adam"* in 1 Corinthians 15:45). Adam encountered his temptation in a beautiful garden, surrounded by every evidence of God's loving provision. Jesus encountered His temptation in a barren wilderness, with wild beasts for companions. (See Mark 1:13.) Adam succumbed to his temptation by eating; Jesus overcame His

IN ITS ESSENCE, SIN IS THE DESIRE
TO BE INDEPENDENT OF GOD.

temptation by fasting. The implications of these comparisons are profound!

Returning to Satan's encounter with Eve, we observe that the tree also presented her with the three basic forms of temptation. It appealed to her appetite—*"the lust of the flesh."* It appealed to her eyes—*"the lust of the eyes."* It appealed to her ego with the promise that it would make her wise and thus set her free from dependence on God—*"the boastful pride of life."*

In its essence, sin is not doing something wrong. Sin is the desire to be independent of God. Whenever this desire appears in us, it spells spiritual danger. In Eve's case, the means by which she hoped to achieve her independence was knowledge—the knowledge of good and evil. This is one means by which people commonly seek independence from God. Other ways are wealth, fame, and power. One of the subtlest ways of all is religion. We can become so religious that we think we no longer need God.

Motivated by her desire for independence, Eve transferred her confidence from God's word to her own senses. As a result, she quickly succumbed to the tree's threefold temptation and partook of its fruit. Then she enticed her husband into doing the same, and both of them together were alienated from God by their disobedience.

In light of the foregoing analysis of Genesis 3:1–6, we are now in a position to sum up the nature of temptation. Faith in the invisible realm of God and His Word is both original and natural for man; unbelief is perverted and unnatural. Temptation has the potential to alienate man from his natural faith in God and His Word. It entices man through his physical senses. Traced to its roots, every temptation is a temptation to disbelieve God. The motive it exploits is the desire to be independent of Him. When temptation is succumbed to, the result it produces is disobedience against God.

THE SENSES APPEAL TO MAN'S SELF-EXALTING EGO, BUT FAITH HUMBLES MAN'S INDEPENDENT NATURE.

FAITH IS THE ANTIDOTE

Faith works in exactly the opposite direction of temptation. Faith requires man to renounce both his confidence in his senses and his egotistical ambition to exalt himself in independence from God. In addition, faith reasserts the supremacy of the invisible realm of God and His Word and requires man to humble himself and acknowledge his dependence on God. Thus, faith undoes the effects of man's fall and opens the way for him to return to his original relationship with God.

Confronted with God's requirement of faith on the one hand and the claims of his senses on the other, man finds himself in a dilemma, caught between two opposing forces. These opposing forces are set forth in Habakkuk 2:4: *"Behold, his soul which is lifted up is not upright in him: but the just shall live by his faith"* (KJV). As we have already noted, the second half of this verse is quoted three times in the New Testament, providing the scriptural basis for justification by faith rather than by works. However, we can see the full scope of the dilemma only when we set the two halves of the verse against one another, viewing them as opposites, each of which excludes the other.

It is important to see that the first half of the verse describes man's soul in its rebellion against God. The original Hebrew words mean, "Behold, his soul is puffed up; it is not upright in him." This corresponds to what John called *"the boastful pride of life"* (1 John 2:16). We might paraphrase Habakkuk 2:4 as follows: "The soul that exalts itself becomes perverted." Man's ego, seeking to exalt himself, rejects the claims of God and His Word and prefers instead to trust his own senses and to strive after independence from God.

The second half of the verse depicts the opposite alternative. The man who makes faith his basis for living humbles himself before God, accepting God's Word as his standard and rejecting confidence in himself and his senses. The senses appeal to man's independent, self-exalting ego, but faith humbles man's ego, saying, in effect, "You are *not* independent. You must depend on God. You can trust your senses only when they agree with God's Word. Your final standard of right and wrong, or truth and error, is not what your senses tell you but what God says in His Word."

Thus, faith cuts away the ground on which the fall took place. The fall made man captive to the sense realm: *"The woman saw that the tree was good for food"* (Genesis 3:6). It exalted man's ego: *"You will be like God"* (verse 5). All that self-exaltation must be undone if we are to live the life of righteousness that is pleasing to God. How is it to be undone? By the faith principle. Faith rejects both the dominion of the senses and the boastful, self-exalting pride of the soul.

In Romans 3:27, Paul pointed out that true faith is incompatible with pride: *"Where then is boasting? It is excluded. By what kind of law? Of works? No, but by a law of faith."* Any kind of religious feeling or activity that leaves room for man's independent, self-exalting egotism is not the expression of valid, scriptural faith.

As you can see, there are two ways of living. Man can reject the idea of dependence on God and trust in himself and his senses alone. Or man can renounce confidence in himself and his senses and trust in what his senses cannot comprehend—God and His Word. By weaning us away from self and the sense realm, faith brings us back to the principle of righteousness that is based on trust in God and His Word. Only this righteousness enables us to live a life that is pleasing to God.

Faith is the antidote to the fall.

SUMMARY

Faith is part of the eternal nature of God. Through His word, spoken in faith, He created the entire universe. As part of his likeness to God, man shares three aspects of the divine nature: the ability to exercise faith, the ability to create, and the ability to speak.

Having created man with the ability to exercise faith, God placed him in a situation where he needed to do so. Adam in the garden did not continue to relate directly to God as a person. Instead, he related to God through the word God had left him— the threefold word of permission, prohibition, and warning.

To alienate Adam from God, Satan approached him indirectly through the "weaker vessel," Eve. He began by undermining Eve's confidence in God's word, by first questioning it and then directly denying it. Then he went on to undermine her confidence in God Himself by suggesting that she and her husband did not need to remain in a position of inferiority but could achieve equality with God by acquiring the knowledge of good and evil. This desire for independence from God is the inner motivation that leads to sin.

In this way, Eve was persuaded to renounce her confidence in the invisible realm of God and His word. She came down instead to the realm of the senses. In the forbidden tree, she was confronted with the three basic forms of temptation: the lust of the flesh, the lust of the eyes, and the boastful pride of life. Operating in the lower realm of the senses, Eve was no longer able to resist the tree's appeal but succumbed to temptation and persuaded her husband to do the same.

Faith reverses the process of temptation that led to man's fall. Faith requires man to renounce both his confidence in his senses and his self-exalting desire to achieve independence from God. Faith also requires man to reaffirm his confidence in the invisible realm of God and His Word. Man's destiny is determined by his response to faith's requirement.

FAITH PROCLAMATIONS AND CORRESPONDING SCRIPTURES

PROCLAMATIONS

1. I walk by faith and not by sight.

2. I will continue in the faith and will not be moved from the hope of the gospel.

3. As Abraham did, I will remain hoping and believing—although it seems impossible—for what God has promised me, without being weakened in the faith.

I notice that the natural circumstances make it impossible, but I do not doubt God's promise. On the contrary, I am strengthened in faith, and by doing so, I give glory to God.

I am persuaded that God is powerful to do what He has promised.

4. My faith does not stand upon the wisdom of men but on the power of God.

5. Therefore, I am not afraid; I believe.

6. By faith, I have boldness to come to God with confidence.

7. I do not throw away my confidence; it will be richly rewarded. I need to patiently do God's will to obtain the promise.

8. The Bible says that no one who puts their faith in Jesus will ever be put to shame or be disappointed.

CORRESPONDING SCRIPTURES (NKJV)

1. Second Corinthians 5:7: *"For we walk by faith, not by sight."*

2. Colossians 1:23: *"If indeed you continue in the faith, grounded and steadfast, and are not moved away from the hope of the gospel which you heard, which was preached to every creature under heaven, of which I, Paul, became a minister."*

3. Romans 4:18–21: *"...who, contrary to hope, in hope believed, so that he became the father of many nations, according to what was spoken, 'So shall your descendants be.' And not being weak in faith, he did not consider his own body, already dead (since he was about a hundred years old), and the deadness of Sarah's womb. He did not waver at the promise of God through unbelief, but was strengthened in faith, giving glory to God, and being fully convinced that what He had promised He was also able to perform."*

4. First Corinthians 2:5: *"...that your faith should not be in the wisdom of men but in the power of God."*

5. Luke 8:50: *"But when Jesus heard it, He answered him, saying, 'Do not be afraid; only believe, and she will be made well.'"*

6. Ephesians 3:12: *"...in whom we have boldness and access with confidence through faith in Him."*

7. Hebrews 10:35–36: *"Therefore do not cast away your confidence, which has great reward. For you have need of endurance, so that after you have done the will of God, you may receive the promise."*

8. Romans 10:11: *"For the Scripture says, 'Whoever believes on Him will not be put to shame.'"*

ABOUT THE AUTHOR

Derek Prince (1915–2003) was born in India of British parents. He was educated as a scholar of Greek and Latin at Eton College and King's College, Cambridge, in England. Upon graduation, he held a fellowship (equivalent to a professorship) in Ancient and Modern Philosophy at King's College. Prince also studied Hebrew, Aramaic, and modern languages at Cambridge and the Hebrew University in Jerusalem. As a student, he was a philosopher and a self-proclaimed agnostic.

While serving in the British Medical Corps during World War II, Prince began to study the Bible as a philosophical work. Converted through a powerful encounter with Jesus Christ, he was baptized in the Holy Spirit a few days later. Out of this encounter, he formed two conclusions: first, that Jesus Christ is alive; second, that the Bible is a true, relevant, up-to-date book. These conclusions altered the whole course of his life, which he then devoted to studying and teaching the Bible as the Word of God.

Discharged from the army in Jerusalem in 1945, he married Lydia Christensen, founder of a children's home there. Upon their marriage, he immediately became father to Lydia's eight adopted daughters—six Jewish, one Palestinian Arab, and one English. Together, the family saw the rebirth of the state of Israel in 1948.

In the late 1950s, they adopted another daughter while Prince was serving as principal of a teachers' training college in Kenya.

In 1963, the Princes immigrated to the United States and pastored a church in Seattle. In 1973, Prince became one of the founders of Intercessors for America. His book *Shaping History through Prayer and Fasting* has awakened Christians around the world to their responsibility to pray for their governments. Many consider underground translations of the book as instrumental in the fall of communist regimes in the USSR, East Germany, and Czechoslovakia.

Lydia Prince died in 1975, and Prince married Ruth Baker (a single mother to three adopted children) in 1978. He met his second wife, like his first wife, while she was serving the Lord in Jerusalem. Ruth died in December 1998 in Jerusalem, where they had lived since 1981.

Until a few years before his own death in 2003 at the age of eighty-eight, Prince persisted in the ministry God had called him to as he traveled the world, imparting God's revealed truth, praying for the sick and afflicted, and sharing his prophetic insights into world events in the light of Scripture. Internationally recognized as a Bible scholar and spiritual patriarch, Derek Prince established a teaching ministry that spanned six continents and more than sixty years. He is the author of more than eighty books, six hundred audio teachings, and one hundred video teachings, many of which have been translated and published in more than one hundred languages. He pioneered teaching on such groundbreaking themes as generational curses, the biblical significance of Israel, and demonology.

Prince's radio program, which began in 1979, has been translated into more than a dozen languages and continues to touch lives. Derek Prince's main gift of explaining the Bible and its teachings in a clear and simple way has helped build a foundation of faith in millions of lives. His nondenominational, nonsectarian approach has made his teaching equally relevant and helpful to people from all racial and religious backgrounds, and his messages are estimated to have reached more than half the globe.

In 2002, he said, "It is my desire—and I believe the Lord's desire—that this ministry continue the work, which God began through me over sixty years ago, until Jesus returns."

Derek Prince Ministries continues to reach out to believers in over 140 countries with Derek's teaching, fulfilling the mandate to keep on "until Jesus returns." This is accomplished through the outreaches of more than forty-five Derek Prince offices around the world, including primary work in Australia, Canada, China, France, Germany, the Netherlands, New Zealand, Norway, Russia, South Africa, Switzerland, the United Kingdom, and the United States. For current information about these and other worldwide locations, visit www.derekprince.org.

Facebook.com/dpmlegacy

Twitter @DPMUSA2

Welcome to Our House!

We Have a Special Gift for You

It is our privilege and pleasure to share in your love of Christian books. We are committed to bringing you authors and books that feed, challenge, and enrich your faith.

To show our appreciation, we invite you to sign up to receive a specially selected **Reader Appreciation Gift**, with our compliments. Just go to the Web address at the bottom of this page.

God bless you as you seek a deeper walk with Him!

WE HAVE A GIFT FOR YOU. VISIT:

whpub.me/nonfictionthx

WHITAKER
HOUSE